HOW THEY

MET

Also by David Friedman:
We Can Be Kind: Healing Our World
One Kindness at a Time

HOW THEY MET

**True Stories of the Power of Serendipity
in Finding Lasting Love**

David Friedman

Published by:
Library Tales Publishing
www.LibraryTalesPublishing.com
www.Facebook.com/LibraryTalesPublishing

For general information on our other products and services, please contact our Customer Care Department at 1-800-754-5016, or fax 917-463-0892. For technical support, please visit www.LibraryTalesPublishing.com

Library Tales Publishing also publishes its books in a variety of electronic formats. Every content that appears in print is available in electronic books.

Dedication

This book is dedicated to my partner in life, Shawn Moninger, who came from out of nowhere when I least expected him, and brought me a life filled with love and spiritual connection that I never could have imagined.

I would like to thank all the wonderful couples and individuals who so generously and inspiringly shared their "How They Met" stories with me and allowed me to share them with you.

"Everything works out in the end.
If it hasn't worked out yet,
then it's not the end."

Author Unknown

Contents

You're Already There, a companion CD to this book
with seventeen songs composed and performed by
David Friedman can be ordered by writing to the
author at MIDDER2000@aol.com or downloaded at
iTunes.com or amazon.com

You're Already There

Trying to sleep, alone in my bed
Thoughts of the future go 'round in my head
How will I find a love of my own?
A love of the kind that I've never known
Don't know where i'm going
Don't know what to do
But I take comfort knowing
That right here and now
You're out in the world
Searching for me too

You're already there waiting for me
Wondering where in the world I could be
You go through the day dreaming your dream
Afraid that it might not come true
While I'm lying here dreaming of you

You're far, far away or just down the street
But surely some day we are destined to meet
I know in my heart you're coming to me
I don't need to know when and where
I'll just turn and one day you'll be there
And maybe we will know
At the first glance, at the first word

Or maybe we'll go slow
Start out as friends
But in the end
A love to last a lifetime will grow
And that will be our story
I can't wait to live our story

So now go to sleep, and I'll do the same
Knowing your heart though I don't know your name
I trust in a plan much higher than me
To bring us together in time
So 'til you appear, I'll picture you here
Remove all the doubt and let go of the fear
And know that the future is fine

You're already there
Waiting for me
So in a funny way
You're already mine

Author's Foreword

A number of years ago, I found myself suddenly and shockingly single after having been in a fifteen-year relationship. Over the next six months, I went through all the normal stages that people tend to go through after this kind of loss; I traveled, told my story to everyone I could think of, renewed old friendships, threw myself into my work, stepped up my therapy, and slowly, with very little success or satisfaction, began to date.

About six weeks after the breakup, I was lying in bed one night feeling sorry for myself, wondering how I would ever have a life, when a very encouraging thought came to me. Being a songwriter, I put that thought into words, and the result was a song, the lyric to which is written above.

As time went by, I began to remember what I had known fifteen years before and forgotten over the years of steady committed relationship—that meeting the right person is something that is, in many ways, very much out of our hands. People had all sorts of advice for me: "Go out and meet everyone you can; Just sit still and it will happen; You've got to be aggressive; Don't be too pushy; When you see a quality you don't want in someone, stop dating them immediately; Be open; Be cautious; Give it time; Get yourself in good shape; Don't change a thing; You have to change something inside you to allow yourself to meet the right person," etc., etc., ad nauseam. But no matter what I did, it seemed to me that it was going to happen when it was going to happen, and the best I could do was be open and take whatever opportunities were being offered to me, whether or not they seemed to have to do with finding the next love of my life. It felt like a pretty helpless position to be in.

Over the months, just for the fun of it, I began asking people who were married or were in longstanding relationships how they met. In each case, there was some element of serendipity or surprise, and I found the stories encouraging, supporting the notion that it would happen for me if I could just live my life and let go. Also encouraging was the fact that meeting the love of one's life did not seem to depend on one's being in particularly good shape, looking good, being successful, being happy at the time, planning, targeting, doing the right thing, or anything else for that matter that one could put one's finger on. In fact, people often met the love of their lives while dressed in dirty old clothes, or while in the middle of a deep depression, or at a time when they absolutely were not looking.

As I listened to story after story, gradually the feeling that I was helpless and that it would never happen for me changed to a sense of wonder and excitement as to when, where, and how it would happen for me. The words of my own song,

"And that will be our story, I can't wait to live our story" ran through my head over and over.

I thought it would be therapeutic for me, during this time, to collect and write down these stories, and then realized that perhaps a book of them would be encouraging for the millions of people who find themselves in similar situations, in love or in anything else that they desire but don't know how to make happen.

Some of these stories were told to me directly by the people who lived them. Others were told to me secondhand. In those cases, I have either changed or omitted the names to protect people's privacy.

Straight, gay, young, old, longtime single, divorced, widowed, looking, not looking—these are stories about ordinary people like you and me, and the ordinary yet extraordinary events that brought them together with their life partner. I hope you enjoy them, find inspiration and encouragement, and perhaps even recognize your own circumstances in them. And whatever you're searching for, be it love, success, healing, money, work, a new home, or a new direction, know that it's entirely possible, no matter what the present circumstances, that you will soon have a new story of your own to tell.

The Stories

Pooper Scooper Romance

Joe was out walking his dog in New York City, and he realized he'd forgotten to bring his pooper scooper. He went to the corner garbage can and picked up a newspaper someone had thrown out, intending to use it to clean up after his dog. The paper was open to the Personals section, and as he picked it up, a particular ad caught his eye. He ripped the ad out of the paper, used the rest for his dog, went home, called the woman who'd placed the ad, and they're married today.

"Maid" for You

Sarah took a look around her house one Saturday and decided it definitely needed cleaning very badly. She put on some old, dirty work clothes and a bandanna and got to work, but soon realized that this was going to be a bigger job than she thought. She pulled out the phonebook, called a temp agency, and asked them to send somebody over to her house to clean it. A short while later, the doorbell rang and a gorgeous man was standing there. He was so good-looking, in fact, that she was sorry she was dressed in such a sloppy cleaning outfit. As it happened, that didn't matter a bit. It turned out that the man at the door was a doctor newly arrived from Africa who hadn't yet gotten his license to practice in the US, and was taking cleaning jobs to make ends meet until his license came through. They are married today.

She Listened to the Fortune Teller

Pat was nineteen years old and in college, but dating a guy from home she liked well enough. Even though there was no real magic or excitement in the relationship, she was actually thinking of getting engaged to him. Just for kicks, she went to a fortune teller. The fortune teller told her that she would meet the man she would marry within the year. She told Pat that his first initial would be either J or G (somehow she seemed to see both), that he was a doctor, and that the first thing she would notice about him would be his laugh. Pat brushed this off as fun but ridiculous, and soon forgot about it. A year later, she was sitting in her dorm suite at college and heard a group of her suitemates and some other friends having a rather raucous conversation across the room. She looked up and noticed that there was one guy who had a really infectious laugh and seemed to be laughing all the time. "Now that's an attractive guy," she thought. Turns out his name was Gerald (with a G), but he usually used the nickname Jerry (with a J). Today, over forty-five years later, he's a doctor and he and Pat have been married for over forty years.

A Foolhardy Trip and a Missed Train

Steve is a Broadway musical director. He had a big show coming up in about five weeks and was pretty nervous about how he was going to prepare for it. All of a sudden, he had the urge to go visit an old friend in Vienna, Austria. Having been a music director myself and knowing how much preparation a Broadway show takes, I told him I couldn't imagine why he would choose to go on a trip at this particular time instead of doing his work, but he was insistent. So off he went to Vienna to visit his friend Amy. After a few days in Vienna, Steve decided to go to Prague for a couple of days. He went to the train station to catch the last train out, only to discover he'd missed it. "Oh well," he thought, "I guess I won't be going to Prague." Having a free evening ahead of him, he decided to see if he could get a ticket to the Wiener Staatsoper (Vienna State Opera). He went down to the box office and—surprise, surprise!—got the last available ticket. He sat down in his seat, and fell in love with the guy sitting next to him. They went out the whole time Steve was in Vienna, and a few months later the guy came over to the US to be with Steve. And that's why Steve went to Vienna.

Midnight Snack in the Pickle Section

Mrs. Gold was in her early sixties and had been widowed for two years. One night she woke up at 3 a.m. and had such a strong yen for pickles that she actually got dressed and went to the open-all-night supermarket to get some. There, in front of the pickle jars, she met a lovely man who ended up being her husband.

They Didn't Let a Little Attitude Stop Them

In 1935, Sylvia was ahead of her time. She owned a retail store and her own car. Mike was delivering a new mattress to one of his customers down the block from Sylvia's store in Brooklyn, and as he pulled up, he watched Sylvia unsuccessfully trying to back her car into a parking space, something she never learned to do. Being a kind of cocky fellow with a dry sense of humor, he walked up to the car and said, "Where did you get your license?" And Sylvia, without a trace of rancor, resentment, or defensiveness, sweetly smiled and said, "If you were a gentleman you would offer to help instead of criticize." To this day, Mike remembers this as the moment he fell in love. He parked the car for her, and asked her for her telephone number. She said, "I don't give my telephone number to strangers," and he said, "Well, if you met me at a dance, would you do it then?" She said, "Yes," and he said, "So let's pretend we're at a dance." She gave him her number and they were together until Sylvia's death fifty-nine years later.

Jewish Mother Knows Best

Carol was concerned about her daughter. True, her daughter was a beautiful and bright woman finishing her doctorate in psychology and seemed by all outside appearances to be a happy, well-adjusted human being. But Carol wasn't fooled. Her daughter was twenty-eight years old, and not only wasn't she married, but as far as Carol could see, she didn't even have any prospects on the horizon. And to add to Carol's concern, her daughter didn't even seem to be at all worried about it. Something had to be done!

When Carol's daughter received an invitation to attend the American Psychological Association conference in Colorado, Carol thought, "Great. She'll get herself out of the house. She'll get a break from her studies. She'll be with her colleagues and will be staying with an old friend. She'll be among people. . . . Maybe she'll meet someone." Her daughter was not as enthusiastic and spent the weeks before the conference complaining. She was feeling overwhelmed by the need to work on her dissertation proposal, and going to the conference would mean a week away from that. Furthermore, it was far away, expensive, intense, and she did not possess as much of a passion for research as she did for the practice of psychology. But with her mother's prodding, she finally resigned herself to attending.

Being a Jewish Mother, Carol usually talked to her daughter pretty frequently—but they hardly spoke when she was in

Colorado. Carol thought it must be because her daughter was busy with the conference, but when Carol started seeing pictures on Instagram of her daughter climbing mountains with two friends, one a very good-looking guy who Carol didn't recognize, Carol began to feel a sense of hope and excitement. As Carol put it, "You wouldn't catch my daughter climbing a mountain unless there was a Saks at the top of it!" Considering herself to be a tactful Jewish Mother, Carol didn't push, but she sensed something was happening because when she did talk to her daughter, her daughter was very giggly and seemed to be having a great time. But her daughter didn't tell Carol much of anything, so Carol remained silent . . . but hopeful.

When her daughter got back to New York, Carol casually asked her who the guy was, and her daughter replied, "Oh, that's Mike." Carol couldn't resist asking if he was nice and if her daughter thought she'd see him again. Her daughter's brief reply was, "Yes, he's nice . . . and I'm seeing him on Tuesday," It was Sunday . . . so that was good.

They went out on that date, and Mike immediately knew that she was the one. It took Carol's daughter a little longer to get on board, but within the year they, along with an adorable dog, were happily living together on the Upper East Side of Manhattan.

Of course, Carol would never insinuate that she made this happen, but being a Jewish Mother from Long Island, she does take a bit of credit for pushing her daughter to attend that conference.

Recipe for Love—Depression, Eating Disorder, Bad Hair, Apathy

Things seemed to be going well for comedienne Julie Halston. She had been in California doing a play and some television guest appearances, while her long-term boyfriend was in New York. Although they were three thousand miles apart for an extended period, Julie had remained true to her boyfriend, even turning down a date from a very well-known, handsome movie star, telling him, "I'm sorry but I'm in a committed relationship back home."

When her TV pilot was over, Julie headed back to New York to star in an Off-Broadway play, do her one-woman show in a club, and move in with her boyfriend. Shortly after she opened in the play, Julie was nominated for a Drama Desk Award.

Unfortunately, just as all this was happening, Julie discovered that her boyfriend was having an affair. Determined to make the relationship work, she tried to stay and work it out, but after a few futile attempts, they decided to call it quits.

Julie went into a tailspin. She had given her New York apartment to a dying friend when she'd moved in with her boyfriend, so she now had no boyfriend and no place to live. She soon became extremely depressed and began developing symptoms of anorexia, but somehow she managed to find a temporary place to live and spent her days sleeping, going to do her shows and going home by herself.

One night, her publicist mentioned that he wanted her to meet his friend, radio interviewer Ralph Howard. Julie informed him in no uncertain terms that the last thing she wanted to do was meet a man. She was absolutely uninterested! After the run of the show, she was going to go to California, by herself, to pursue her career. At least there people seemed to like her.

Unbeknownst to Julie, and in spite of her protestations, her publicist asked Ralph if he was available (yes, he had just stopped dating a woman in Washington, DC) and brought him to see her show. Although Ralph and Julie didn't meet in person that night, Ralph was very impressed with her performance and asked Julie's publicist if he might interview Julie. Julie was not interested, but when her publicist forced the issue (mostly to get Julie out of the house during the day, as he was worried about her health and state of mind), Julie reluctantly accepted.

On the day of the interview, her hair a mess, wearing no makeup and a pajama top (she could care less), she went to the studio. When Ralph opened the door, she was pleasantly surprised at how cute he was and how comfortable she felt with him.

"Hmm," she thought, "maybe a little affair before I leave for California would be nice, nothing serious of course." She found herself sitting at attention and on her best behavior during the interview. But she left with no plans to see Ralph again.

Julie's publicist called and insisted she come see a show he was involved with on a certain night because that was the night Ralph was going to be there. Again, reluctantly, Julie said OK. However, when she got there and saw Ralph sitting across the room, for reasons she couldn't understand, she found herself climbing over chairs and pushing people out of the way to grab a seat near him. She suddenly had the sinking feeling in her stomach that this would not just be an affair but was something more serious. And she didn't want that!

She and Ralph had a pleasant evening together, and a few days later she left for California. When she arrived in California there was a message from Ralph welcoming her to California (he was still in New York), and while she was out there they spoke every day on the phone. But Julie was making her life in California and Ralph was on the radio in New York, so it seemed unlikely much would happen.

As fate would have it, the development deal Julie was working on in Los Angeles became contingent upon her appearing in a show in New York, so before long she found herself back there. She and Ralph still hardly knew each other, but out of the blue Ralph invited her on a vacation to Aruba and she found herself accepting. Four months later, Ralph had a heart-to-heart talk with her about having to take a leap and get serious. That night they went to see the movie Frankie and Johnnie, which was about just that, and Julie found herself weeping through the whole film. The next day they got engaged and they've been happily married for years.

Love at First Sight

When Al was in his early twenties, in the late 1930s, he was a great dancer. He would go to clubs in New York, New Jersey, and Connecticut and dance the night away. He had beautiful dancing partners in all these places, but none of them ever clicked for him as being the girl he could get serious with. When he went to the army, he was transferred to Arkansas.

In the evenings, some of the men would cross the state border into Tennessee and dance with the girls who were brought down there, with chaperones of course, to dance with the soldiers. At his first dance, he spent the evening watching a girl on the dance floor and said to himself, "That's the one." He says he'll never forget the feeling and doesn't know why she was the one. She just looked right to him. As her bus was leaving after the dance, Al jumped on the back and through the open window asked her out. They immediately began dating and spending evenings dancing together.

Before he went overseas he gave her a ring and he said, "If things don't work out well for me overseas, throw away the ring and start over. If they do work out well, marry me when I get back." Al came back, they got married, and remained married until her death in 1990.

Heartbreaks in Common Brought Them Together (Very Slowly)

Marianne was in her early forties, was married to a very wealthy oilman, and was the mother of seven children. During a fairly routine discussion one evening, her husband shockingly informed her that he no longer wanted to be married and left. Suddenly, she was the single parent of seven kids, and her whole life turned upside down. Although she felt extremely humiliated and frightened, Marianne quickly determined that she was going to face the challenge in front of her and raise those children. Meeting someone was the last thing on her mind.

A couple of years after her husband left, Marianne decided to go back to school. She was taking a course in Ethnic and Economic Backgrounds, and Joe was her teacher. In this course, students had to get up and tell their life story, so Joe knew a good bit about Marianne's history. Joe also thought she wrote thoughtful, intelligent, well-written papers. During that year, Joe's wife, who had been going through a long illness, died. The class knew about it, and Marianne sent him a card.

At the end of the last class, Marianne and Joe were talking, and Marianne told him about her husband leaving her with the seven kids. After Marianne left the room, Joe turned to someone standing next to him and said, "My God, how could he leave a woman like her?" Over the next six months they would pass each other in the cafeteria and say hello. One day, on a whim, Marianne approached Joe and invited him to the ballet. He accepted. On their first date Joe was really strange, talking about other women and seeming not to be interested in Marianne at all. Marianne left that date thinking, "Forget about him, he's really weird." About six months later, Marianne's phone rang and it was Joe. At first she didn't even call him back, but then he called again, she went out with him, and they married soon after.

Dancing in the Automat

For those too young to remember, Horn & Hardart (better known as "The Automat") was a very popular New York restaurant chain. It was unique because the walls were lined with little glass doors behind which were sandwiches, salads, desserts and drinks. You put a nickel, dime, or quarter in the slot next to a particular door, it opened, and voila, you had your meal. No waiter, no check, just "Automatic" service.

Gene had just returned home from World War II and was eating in the Horn & Hardart in Manhattan. He saw a young woman eating with her sisters and went over and asked her to dance. It was a strange and unusual thing to do in a fast food restaurant, but she said yes, and not long after she said yes again when he asked her to marry him.

Take My Brother, Please!!!

Bill and his brother John were walking down the street in the small town in which they lived, when they came across a group of pretty young girls. John went up to the girls and asked, "Who wants to marry my brother Bill?" Dee raised her hand and said. "I will." And she did!

"Hey Minister! Who's the Babe in the Pew?"

Joe was the new music minister at a church in Texas. He was sitting on the dais one Sunday morning with the Head Minister during services when a young woman in a purple dress walked in from the back of the church and sat down. Joe, totally knocked out by this woman, leaned over to the minister and mouthed, "Who's the babe?" "What?" said the minister, unable to make out what he was saying. "Who's the babe?" "What?" "Who's the really hot babe in the purple dress who just walked in and sat down?" "That's my daughter!" Oops. Anyway, it turned out the girl was the minister's daughter and that she didn't very often come to church. Joe decided that the way to meet her was to get her to join the choir. A novel approach, walking up to a girl you're interested in and saying, "You look like an alto, why don't you be in the choir?" But she joined and they got friendlier, and one day Pamela asked her father if it would be alright to invite Joe to the house for dinner. Her father said yes, but for some reason Pamela didn't follow through. But Pamela's mother went to Joe and told him that Pamela had asked, which gave Joe the courage to ask her out. They're married today.

Obligated to Meet

Phyllis was twenty-one and went to Israel to work on an ulpan, a work farm for foreigners wanting to help Israel. Her brother-in-law, who had decided that Phyllis would marry Betzalel (her brother-in-law hadn't told Phyllis this, and Phyllis had never met Betzalel) told Phyllis she had to look Betzalel up at the King David Hotel to send his regards. Dutifully, Phyllis called Betzalel and conveyed her brother-in-law's regards. Betzalel, in an aloof sort of way that some might say is indigenous to Israeli men, said, "Who are you?" He decided they were obligated to meet, and he went out to the ulpan where Phyllis was working. This was a little uncomfortable for him since for an Israeli to go out to an ulpan was often construed as the Israeli trying to hook up with an American to procure his rights both in Israel and America. But he went and invited her out on Friday night. Phyllis had already been invited to a Shabbat dinner at someone's house, but Betzalel insisted they go out afterward. They went out and the next Friday Betzalel's mother invited Phyllis to her house for Shabbat, and that was the beginning of the relationship. They've been married for over forty years.

If It's Meant to Be, It's Meant to Be

Ron had just broken up a long-term relationship with a man who was quite a bit older and very much more accomplished and further along in his career than he was. He was now alone, and his friends suggested that he make a list of all the qualities he wanted in a man and put it up somewhere where he could look at it every day. Ron did that, writing down a specific description of the attributes of his dream lover, and put the list on his refrigerator. Nothing seemed to happen, so after a few months he took it off.

After several years of being by himself, Ron got involved with a man who was certainly not his dream lover, but the relationship lasted a long time. He and his boyfriend were in therapy but there was a certain complacency, joint property, and an intertwined lifestyle that made them both feel that even though this relationship was not really working, it would go on.

Ron was standing by the subway entrance on 86th Street in Manhattan saying goodnight to a man with whom he'd just had a business meeting. Ron found himself wondering if this man was gay or not . . . he just couldn't tell. All of a sudden a very attractive tall man walked by and looked right at them as he passed. Ron said to the man he was with: "I think you just got cruised," and the man responded, "Ooh, honey, I don't think it was me he was cruising." Ron smiled thinking "Okay, now I know this guy's gay."

The man who had cruised Ron went into Gristedes. Ron said goodnight to his business associate and walked down into the subway. The train was slow in coming, but there was a singer performing on the platform and Ron really got into it and was standing there enjoying the performance when he realized the handsome man who'd cruised him was standing near him. This made Ron really nervous so he didn't look—he just kept listening to the music. When the train finally arrived, Ron made a point to see which car the guy was going into and proceeded to go into a different one. He sat down and thought, "Whew, glad I don't have to deal with that." A few minutes later he looked up and realized that the man was now standing near him in his car. (The interesting thing is that Lars, the man who Ron thought was cruising him, does not remember going after Ron, switching cars to be near him or following him in any way.)

Ron surreptitiously began to glance up at the man, trying to find things he didn't like about him. Didn't like the shoes. Didn't like the tie. He said nothing to the man—he was just too unnerved at the thought of talking to this stranger on the subway—but something kept drawing the two of them together. He was on the local train, and at 34th Street he thought he heard the conductor announce that the train was now going express. He had been told to take the local train, so he got off the train. (Actually, he was going to 14th Street, which would have been the next express stop, but he got confused about directions and thought he needed to get off.) He was standing on the platform and he noticed that the man had gotten off too. Then he heard the conductor announce that the next stop was 28th Street, which meant that the train actually was a local, so he got back on. He noticed out of the corner of his eye that the man had gotten back on too. (Again, the fascinating thing about this is that Lars has no memory of following Ron or cruising him or anything. He was just going about his business, not even noticing where Ron was.)

At 14th Street, both men got off the train, Ron stood on the platform trying to figure out which exit he should go to, and the man went toward an exit at the end of the platform. As Ron was standing there he saw the man turn around . . . the exit he was going toward was closed, and the man was heading toward Ron on his way to the other exit. As the man passed Ron, something made Ron reach into his pocket, grab his business card, hand it to the man and say, "Call me." The man said nothing, did not give Ron his number, just took the card and kept walking.

Even though Ron was still in his relationship, for some reason he was very excited. The next day he came into work and asked his secretary if anyone had called. The secretary said, "Yes, Bob called." "Bob," thought Ron. "Hm. That's a nice name. Could it be him?" Ron asked, "Did you get his number?" and the secretary said, "He didn't leave one." Ron went into a whole tirade, saying, "How could you not get his number?!" The secretary looked so taken aback at this outburst that Ron, who had never shared any of the details of his personal life with his secretary, told her the whole story. She was very intrigued and into it, but informed him that she hadn't gotten Bob's number because it was Bob, their accountant from downstairs, who had called.

For the next five days, both Ron and his secretary waited anxiously for a call from the mystery man. The call never came.

Ron's relationship dragged on. They were in couples counseling and Ron even brought up the mystery man in a session, but there was such a sense of inertia and settledness in their relationship that it didn't even seem to ruffle his partner. Over the next year and a half, the relationship continued to drag on, but clearly there was nothing left of it and only familiarity and a sense of "nowhere else to go" were keeping them together.

Ron left his job and moved to another one. A year and a half after the subway encounter, Ron's secretary from his old job got a call. "Hello, this is Lars, is Ron there?" "I'm sorry, Ron doesn't work here anymore," was her reply. "Thank you," Lars said, and was ready to hang up. Now this was a government agency and their policy was not to give out forwarding numbers of employees who had left. But the secretary had remembered the story of the mystery man on the subway, and even though Lars had said nothing to indicate that he was that mystery man from a year and a half ago, the secretary said, "Would you like the number where Ron works now?" Lars, after hesitating, said, "Okay." Ron was sitting at work when the phone rang.

When Ron answered the phone, he heard a voice on the other end say, "This is Lars, I'm the man you gave your card to on the subway a year and a half ago." Now Ron knew that quite a few friends of his knew about the subway incident and he assumed someone was pulling his leg. "Oh, helloooo Laaaars," he said in an extremely sarcastic voice. But when Lars began to talk to him and related things about the incident that only Lars could have known, Ron realized he was really talking to the guy. "What took you so long to call?" Ron asked. Actually, Lars had at first not wanted to call because he assumed that he wouldn't be interested in a guy who makes a habit of giving his business card out on the subway. He'd then lost the card and was cleaning out some things and found it in a box. His friends had been pressuring him to be more aggressive in looking for a boyfriend . . . he'd been single for a while, doing a bit of casual dating but nothing serious, and his friends were warning him that if you remain single too long it becomes a way of life and your relationship muscles shrivel up and atrophy. So when he found the card, he figured he'd go through the motions and take the initiative, even though it seemed ridiculously unlikely that it would lead to anything.

Lars was shocked that Ron even remembered him, thinking that Ron must give out his card on the subway all the time, but as they talked, he realized that Ron had never done such a thing before or since. They talked for forty minutes and at the end, Lars gave Ron his home number, his work number, his address, and his cell phone number. Ron said, "Well, you have my work number" and left it at that. Now Lars was paying attention, so he said, "Something is strange here. Are you involved with someone?" "Well, sort of." said Ron. "Well, if you ever become totally available, give me a call." was Lars' reply. A few weeks later, Ron and his boyfriend finally decided to split up. Ron actually called his former boyfriend, the one who was older and very successful, and asked if he could use the empty apartment he kept in New York. (The ex-boyfriend had moved to L.A.) His ex said fine, and Ron moved out of the apartment he was in and into this one. The first call he made was to Lars.

Lars spent about two weeks having long conversations with Ron, making sure that he would not just be a rebound relationship. They then got together, and the rest is history. They've been partners for the last thirty years.

Oh, and by the way, the list Ron had placed on his refrigerator years before . . . described Lars to a tee.

It Took Five Disasters to Bring Them Together

Without the simultaneous occurrence of five disasters, Rene and Peter would have never gotten together. Rene had spent several years caring for her ailing father who was suffering from Alzheimer's Disease. Shortly after he died, her mother developed the same disease. Rene, who had been single for a long time, was the only child really in a position to give up her life as she knew it and care for her mother. After several years during which Rene spent most of her time shuttling between her home in New York, her mother's homes in Florida and New Jersey, and her brother's home in Los Angeles, where her mother often stayed, Rene's mother finally died.

The next day, when Rene picked up the phone to call one of her oldest and dearest friends, Penny, to tell her her mother had died, Penny informed Rene that she had just been diagnosed with stage 4 lymphoma. Rene had always been a natural caretaker. In addition to taking care of both her dying parents she had also spent many years volunteering at Memorial Sloan Kettering Cancer Center and continues to do so to this day. So even though her mother had just died, Rene volunteered to come to New Jersey to accompany Penny to all her chemotherapy sessions and help take care of her during her treatment.

While this was going on, Penny's brother Peter was having his own problems. Peter lived in Florida, and after a fifteen-year marriage, his wife told him that she wanted a divorce. At the same time, in the course of a one-month period, two of Peter's best friends committed suicide. Then Peter got the call that his sister had cancer. Like Rene, Peter volunteered to come up to New Jersey to take care of her.

Rene had known Peter slightly from high school, but basically she'd just known him as Penny's older brother. Rene and Peter spent a lot of time sitting in chemo waiting rooms and hanging out and helping Penny at her home. Rene began to notice that she felt really comfortable with Peter, although she wasn't feeling any romantic feelings. But as time went on and they began to spend more time together, feelings started to grow between them. It was a long, complex courtship, both were recovering from a lot of pain and trauma, but they took their time, often not being in contact for months as they each took care of their personal business in their own cities, going as slowly as they needed to with each other. After about nine months, a love that was stronger than either of them had ever experienced blossomed and they are now married.

Office Romance

Michael was the extremely successful owner of a very large company. Lisa worked running one of the departments. They hardly knew each other. One day, Michael was giving someone a tour of the company facilities and when they got to Lisa's department, the man who was receiving the tour said, "Is she your wife?" That was a really strange thing to say out of the blue, but Michael found himself saying, "No, but I wish she was."

Now Michael had recently been through a very painful divorce and he says that Lisa looked like a much younger version of his ex-wife, although considering how rancorous that divorce had been, it's surprising that he would have had feelings for anyone who looked like her. Perhaps Lisa was his "type." At any rate, one thing led to another and they began to go out.

But as they got more serious, Michael's distrust and his memory of past failed relationships made him reluctant to want to commit. Michael was a good deal older than Lisa and felt they wanted different things. Lisa was pressuring him for more commitment. Finally, Lisa gave him an ultimatum, and when he didn't rise to it, Lisa left.

For the next period of time, they were apart and Michael began to date other women. Being a very wealthy man, he would drive up in an antique Bentley, pick up his date, drive to the airport where they would board his private Gulfstream jet, fly over to Martha's Vineyard or some such place for dinner, and fly back. As Michael tells it, by the second date many women would be falling in love with him, telling him how sexy he was and how anxious they were to make a commitment. Michael was astute enough to realize that these women were not falling in love with him but rather with the material things he was providing.

During this time, Lisa had worked very hard to get over Michael. She went through months of tears and pain and finally felt she had let go and was ready to move on. Then, one day, after nine months of separation, the phone rang and it was Michael. She couldn't imagine why he was calling. Michael told her that, after months of empty dating, he had realized that Lisa was the one who had loved him for himself and not for his money and that he was now willing to make the commitment and marry her. They've been together ever since.

41

Two Bar Stories

In a Bar

I met two people in a restaurant the other day. She's forty, he's sixty, they've been married less than a year, and amazingly enough, it's a first marriage for both. They happily own a restaurant in Nantucket together, as well as having two careers in New York. Since I collect stories about how people met, I asked her to tell me theirs. "How did you meet?" I asked. "In a bar," was her reply.

Sometimes it's just that simple.

A Pickup

On September 22, 1990, Russell went out to a bar in Wilmington, North Carolina, met Anthony, brought him home, and they've been together ever since. They were legally married on September 5, 2013 in Potomac, MD.

He Went to That Party He Didn't Want to Go To

Burgess had had a horrible breakup with his former boyfriend, when he discovered that he was having an affair with the husband of a woman friend of theirs. After that, Burgess didn't date for almost five years, and was just starting to date casually when he was invited to a New Year's Eve party. He didn't particularly want to go, but at 10 p.m. got himself dressed and went. Dan had been invited to the same party. Also being single and, like Burgess, casually dating someone, Dan hadn't really felt like going either, but decided that he would go, help the host, and leave early. The moment Burgess walked in, Dan says that he saw him across the room and remembers thinking, "This is a man I'd want to settle in and spend the rest of my life with." Burgess remembers also spotting Dan across the room and thinking him attractive, but not really being interested since Dan was not young, hot, dark, and Cuban, the type Burgess was usually attracted to. However, they did get to talking and didn't stop the whole evening. After the party they went out to a coffee shop and continued to talk until three in the morning. They talked about the guys they'd begun to date, about their problems, and about life, with no discussion of their dating or anything like that, but just as new friends.

Over the course of the next six months, they became fast friends. Sporadically, they would spend a lot of time with each other, talking, doing things together, having meals, and in time they grew to be really close friends, still not making the move toward becoming more. Then one day, as Burgess tells it, Dan called him and said, "I'd like to cook for you." Now Dan is a wonderful cook, so Burgess immediately accepted. They decided they would have a picnic by the sea, and during the course of the meal, as the sun set over the ocean, Burgess noticed that Dan had taken his hand. Dan proceeded to tell him that he couldn't hold out much longer and that he hadn't wanted to push or rush him, but he'd been in love with him and extremely attracted to him since the night they'd met. Burgess was taken by surprise and hadn't really allowed himself to think that way, but he and Dan went back to Dan's house and made love, and have been together ever since, which is over thirty years now. And Burgess tells me their lovemaking and their closeness are as fresh and new as they were all those years ago.

Good Morning Heartache

Ervin Drake, world-renowned songwriter of such hits as "I Believe" and the Broadway musical Golden Boy, was nineteen when he met the love of his life, who was sixteen. At the time, Ervin was a starving songwriter who was having a lot of trouble finding success. The love of his life came from a well-to-do, socially prominent family. Though they were madly in love, she was concerned about settling down with him, so she broke up with him to play the field. Ervin was devastated to the point of contemplating suicide. So devastated in fact, that he wrote the scathing song "Good Morning Heartache," which became his first big hit.

Ervin and the love of his life each went on to marry other people. Coincidentally, they both ended up living in Great Neck, Long Island. After twenty-five years, Ervin's wife died. Around the same time, the love of his life's husband also died. Hearing about Ervin's wife's death, she called to console him and they arranged to meet for dinner. Right then and there they realized that they'd always been soulmates. They got married very soon after, and stayed married for the rest of their lives. So her breaking up with Ervin handed him his career, and they ended up together in the end.

An Angel in Canine Form

Linda, an aspiring young actress just out of college, had been dating a Hollywood celebrity for four years and had thought that this was the man she would be with for the rest of her life. However, as it gradually began to dawn on her that her boyfriend was unable to be faithful to one woman, she reluctantly realized that she had to end the relationship.

On the day she moved out, she arrived at her new house to find a dog sitting in her driveway. The dog had no collar and no tags, so she went into the house and left it outside, figuring it would go away.

As soon as she went into the house, the dog came up onto the porch, jumped up on a table, curled up, and went to sleep.

45

(She realized later that the dog was sleeping on the table so it could look into the house and see her.)

Day after day, the dog would be parked in front of her house, and night after night, the dog would sleep on the porch. Finally, Linda decided to take the dog in. She named him Charlie.

Linda took Charlie to the vet to have him checked out, and discovered, to her dismay, that Charlie had a serious heart condition. "I'm afraid this dog has about three days to live." was the vet's prognosis. "We can try and give him medication, but I don't think it will help."

Linda had no money at the time (she was basically subsisting on small fees she would receive from acting jobs here and there) and could not afford the medication. The vet, seeing her upset, offered to give Charlie the treatment and medication for free if Linda would allow the vet to use the dog for a research project after its death.

She took Charlie home, and Charlie lived healthily for three more years! During that time, Linda and Charlie were inseparable. She got a job doing presentations for an advertising company, and Charlie, who was never on a leash but would follow her everywhere, would actually go on stage with her and sit by her for all the presentations.

Linda began dating someone else, but not particularly seriously, because she felt so burnt by her previous relationship. She also befriended a man at work named Bob. They worked side by side constantly and had a wonderful collaborative friendship, but there was no thought of anything more. They were just friends who liked each other a lot and worked well together.

As time went on, Bob began to be interested in Linda as someone he could like as more than just a friend, but because Linda was seeing someone else, Bob felt that nothing could happen between them.

One day, Linda and Bob had a serious problem with their boss. They had done a presentation and the boss was dissatisfied and became unreasonably enraged. On the bus ride back to the office, the boss was screaming at Bob, berating him publicly and threatening to fire him.

When they got back to the office, Bob went to a restaurant next door to try and cool off. Linda found herself waiting around for Bob to make sure he was alright. Finally, she went into the restaurant and they decided to go to a different restaurant and have dinner. During that dinner, as they talked and talked and talked, they both had an unspoken realization that something had changed between them and that something romantic seemed to be in the air.

A few days later, Bob decided to take the chance and asked Linda out on a date. He took her to dinner and to see Beatlemania, and then took her home. He couldn't come in though, because he was highly allergic to dogs and Linda still had Charlie. But he kissed her goodnight, and Linda reports that after that one kiss, she closed the door, slid down to the floor and thought, "My God. This is the one."

But still reeling from her four-year relationship-gone-wrong, and seeing her relationship with the man she was presently dating falling away, Linda was reluctant to get involved, so she held Bob at bay. She told Bob that she didn't want to get serious, and anyway, she had a dog and Bob was allergic to dogs. Basically, out of fear, she used Charlie as an excuse to not get closer.

Bob responded by saying he understood and they should remain just friends.

And then . . . Charlie died.

A few days later, Linda and Bob were working late in the office and were the only ones left. Bob asked Linda if she would like to grab some Chinese food, making sure to emphasize that this was not a date, just dinner between two friends. Linda accepted the invitation, they went to dinner, they went back to Linda's house (where there was no longer a dog), and Bob never left.

They've been married for thirty-five years.

It's very clear in Linda's mind and heart that Charlie was her guardian angel. He showed up out of nowhere on the day

Linda's relationship ended, kept her company through her years healing, living far past the time he was supposed to, and "stepped out" when Linda was taken care of and ready for the love of her life.

That dog "knew" something.

Don't Assume

This story was told to me by my friend Mel. It's not exactly a "How They Met" story, but it so supports the "you never know" theme that I wanted to include it.

Over thirty years ago, Mel was best friends with a guy who was "absolutely gorgeous." So gorgeous in fact, that Mel never gave a romantic relationship a thought, even though he secretly pined for this guy. Being sensible and knowing that a knockout like this would never give someone like him a second glance, Mel contented himself with a wonderful friendship. They were, in fact, almost inseparable, they hung out a lot, the guy always invited Mel places, they had great dinners and spent a lot of time enjoying each other's company and talking about life. Ultimately Mel was grateful to be friends with this guy, even though he knew it could never be more.

Eventually they drifted apart, and after not too long Mel met Paul and began a relationship that has lasted to this day. He had long ago forgotten about his gorgeous friend, until one day he ran into him in the supermarket and they got to talking. His friend was also in a long-term relationship, and as they began to share the stories of their lives, Mel's friend looked at him and said, "Were you aware of how much in love I was with you?" Mel replied, "WHAT?!?!" His friend continued, "I tried everything to get you to notice me, calling you up all the time, going places with you, but you seemed so uninterested in a romantic relationship that I eventually gave up."

Thirty years later both are content to be where they are with the partners they are with, but it goes to show you, "Never assume! And never underestimate your own attractiveness."

She Didn't Catch the Bouquet, But She Did Catch a Husband

Victoria's close friends were getting married and she was going to the wedding without a date.

Victoria had been dating a guy for some time but he had neglected to tell her one small detail about himself. He was married.

About two weeks prior to her friends' wedding (to which Victoria had invited her "boyfriend") Victoria was at work (she was a producer for a morning talk show in New York

City) when she received a call from a woman who told her she was her "boyfriend's" next-door neighbor and that she felt Victoria should know that her "boyfriend" was married. Apparently, so as not to get caught by his wife, Victoria's "boyfriend" had set up a phone line in his next-door neighbor's house, his next-door neighbor being a close pal of his. When Victoria would call, unbeknownst to her, she was calling an answering machine in the neighbor's house. The neighbor would then go next door, notify Victoria's "boyfriend" that Victoria had called, her "boyfriend" would go next door, and call Victoria back from that phone. The guys were pulling it off until the neighbor's wife got wind of what was going on and felt compelled to tip Victoria off.

A few minutes after Victoria found out the truth, her "boyfriend" called her at the office. Victoria worked in a large open room with a lot of people sitting at desks nearby, so all of her coworkers were privy to Victoria's top-of-her-lungs tirade where she reamed him out for deceiving her, ending the conversation with, "And you were lousy in bed!"

Now, in addition to not having a boyfriend, Victoria had another social dilemma. She was scheduled to go to her friends' Pat and Chas's wedding in less than two weeks, and she now didn't have a date. The wedding was going to be a very expensive and fancy affair at the Union Club, and Victoria knew that they were paying a lot of money per plate. So she called Pat and asked if she should bring a friend or relative as a date so the table arrangements wouldn't get messed up, or if she should just come alone and save them the cost of the extra plate. Pat said, "Come alone. We're going to have a single's table, so you'll be fine."

At the same time, Tony was having a similar problem. Tony, born and raised in New Zealand, had come to Aspen to ski for a season and liked it so much that he stayed for five years, working as a ski instructor and housesitting for the rich and famous. Chas, also an avid skier, was working in Aspen as a sommelier. Tony and Chas hit it off and became fast friends.

Fast forward a number of years: Chas had moved to New York, and Tony was now living in northern New Jersey at Great Gorge, working at the former Playboy Club which had been converted to timeshares. Tony had been dating a girl and Chas invited him to come to the wedding with her, but two weeks before the wedding, Tony and his girlfriend broke up. Tony called Chas with the exact same concern that Victoria had had. "Should I bring someone else to hold the place, or come alone?" Chas told Tony not to worry. They had a singles table and it would be fine for him to come alone.

Although Victoria had been very friendly with Pat for years, and Tony had been very friendly with Chas for years, Victoria and Tony had never met.

Tony and Victoria were both seated at the singles table, though not next to each other. (They later found out that Chas and

Pat had assumed that the two of them would never get along, so they seated them next to other, more "suitable" people.) Victoria was seated next to an Italian guy who she found to be snobby and off-putting, and they put Tony across the table next to a girl who he didn't like either.

Everyone was dancing, and suddenly, in this very fancy Park Avenue club, the air conditioning broke down. It being a formal wedding, with all the men in tuxedos and all the women dressed to the nines, it got very hot in there very quickly. The club was on the first floor, so they opened all the windows to try to at least create a cross-breeze.

Tony took his jacket off and was sitting on the windowsill to get some air. (The club was on the first floor, so there wasn't any danger of falling out the window.) While Victoria was dancing, and really beginning to feel uncomfortably hot, Tony caught her eye from the windowsill and beckoned her to come over. Victoria gave him a look as if to say, "Me? Who? What?" since she didn't even know this guy, but he nodded as if to say, "Yes." So she thought, "Well, I am really hot and he's sitting next to an open window, so I might as well partake of the breeze."

Victoria walked over and said, "Are you talking to me?" to which Tony said, "Yeah, you." The moment she heard him speak, Victoria said, "Oh, where are you from, Australia or New Zealand?" Tony said, "New Zealand," and Victoria said,

"Oh, where men are men and sheep are nervous." Tony got a good laugh out of that, and Victoria said, "I just got back from New Zealand." Tony didn't believe her, telling her, "No way! You're a city girl." (She was dressed in a very dressy sequined black dress and heels, and did, indeed, look like a city girl.) Victoria proceeded to inform him that she had spent her trip driving a camper van all around the country. Tony, a country guy who rarely even came into Manhattan, still didn't believe her, so he began to grill her. "What was your favorite place in New Zealand?" "Oh, definitely Queenstown." Victoria began describing specific things and places she had loved, and finally Tony said, "OK. I guess you really have been to New Zealand."

They began chatting and laughing, and in the course of their conversation—since it was so hot—they convinced themselves that there must be a pool somewhere in this fancy club and set out to look for it. They didn't find one, but they did find a room with a pool table, and as they were leaning against it talking, Tony kissed Victoria. Victoria, feeling the sparks start to fly, said, "We'd better get back to the party."

As the wedding started to wind down, Tony said, "Why don't we go back to your apartment." To which Victoria said, "Oh no. We haven't had a proper date yet. You have to at least take me for a drink." Tony took her to a bar across the street from her apartment, and when they sat down and ordered, Victoria said, "I've got to ask you at least twenty questions." She got through about ten questions and then said, "I just met you.

I have to be able to trust you. Give me your wallet. Let me go through your wallet." Tony handed her his wallet. There were no pictures of girlfriends, no drugs and no condoms. There was something about this guy that Victoria just instinctively trusted, so she took him home with her and he never left.

They were married soon after in a beautiful wedding in Grand Cayman Island, and it's been twenty-seven years and they're still happily together.

While Victoria and Tony had been out of the room at the wedding, the bride had thrown the bouquet. One of Victoria's girlfriends later told her, "I caught the bouquet." To which Victoria responded, "Yeah. But I caught the man."

The Direct Approach

Anne, a successful Broadway actress/singer who starred in such shows as Cyrano, Les Misérables, Victor/Victoria, and The Phantom of the Opera, suddenly found herself widowed at a young age. For a while, she and her seven-year-old daughter stayed in New York, Anne starring in "Phantom" while her daughter performed in "Les Miz" right next door. But it soon became apparent that Anne and her daughter needed a break to gather themselves, heal, and grieve, so they left New York and moved to California to live with Anne's mother, taking

Anne completely out of the Broadway environment where she had lived and worked for so many years.

After a period of time, Anne's therapist and others around her encouraged her to start dating. As Anne describes it, "When I started dating, I used a lot of online dating services. I was very open to meeting different kinds of people, and I sort of had the philosophy that I'd been in show business my whole life, had pretty much only dated people in show business, and it would be really interesting to meet people outside of that world. So I met people who did all kinds of different things, but nothing really clicked. I'd go out on one date, a couple of dates, even date someone for six weeks or a few months, but I didn't find anyone who seemed like they were going to be worth any sort of compromise."

So consciously trying to meet someone and using all the tools available didn't seem to be working.

After a number of years, Anne decided it was time to move back to the New York area, so she and her daughter flew East and settled into a home in Westchester, a suburb just north of the City. Anne was not dating anyone at the time and was no longer using online dating services, but a few friends set her up with people, and after going out on a couple of dates, Anne had a revelation. She thought, "You know what? I'm done. I'm really done. I don't want to date any more. I've met so many people, some really nice people, but nothing is clicking. I'm very self-sufficient, I'm very happy being single, being a single mom, I love my life with my daughter, I have a horse, I love my horse, I love where we live, I'm able to provide for us, I don't need more. And maybe you only get a couple of really great loves in your life, and maybe I've had that and it's just not in the cards for me. So I quit. With contentment. And I was really good with it. I loved my life, my life was really great, I didn't feel lonely, I didn't feel compromised, I didn't feel like I was lacking anything. I had great friends, many from show business, where I had developed incredible friendships with so many people I'd met through the years and become very close to, as well as great girl-friends and man-friends. So my life was very, very full and that's where I was at."

So . . . Anne often made concert appearances with symphonies, and she was invited by Marvin Hamlisch to sing for him at the New Jersey State Theatre with several other Broadway stars. The concert was about two hours' drive from her home, and part of the evening was a black-tie reception after the concert to honor the CEO of Johnson & Johnson. Anne told her agent that since it was a two-hour drive, a sitter was watching her daughter, and since Anne didn't like driving late at night, she wouldn't be staying for the reception. At first her agent said, "Fine, no problem," but then called back an hour later to say. "Everyone's going to the black-tie dinner, you're the only one who's not going, Marvin's going, you need to go." So Anne said, "OK, I'll show up, I'll go for like twenty minutes, I'll sit at the table, I'll talk to everyone who's at my table, but then I am going to have to excuse myself and leave."

Anne sang the concert and went to the reception where she sat at a table next to Montego Glover, who was one of the other Broadway stars on the bill, and chatted with a group of lovely people who were sitting with them. Out of the corner of her eye, Anne noticed a gentleman, with a woman with him, approaching her . . . Anne remembers thinking, "Oh, he's so handsome. Obviously he's with his wife. The good ones are always taken!"

As the man got to the table, he leaned forward and said to both Anne and Montego, "I just wanted to tell you what a fantastic performance both of you gave. You were terrific: you lifted everybody's spirits." He then looked directly at Anne and said, "Are you single?" Kind of taken aback, Anne said, "Yes." To which he said, "Do you have a boyfriend?" to which Anne said, "No." To which he said, "How do I apply for that position?" To which Anne said, "Well, why don't you sit down and I'll see if I'm taking applications."

Montego, being an actress who knew how to take a cue, immediately stood up, said, "I have to go make a phone call," and left the table, leaving her seat vacant for the gentleman to sit down.

So he sat down and they began to chat. Anne explained to him that she would be leaving shortly because she needed to get home, since she had a daughter at home and was a single parent with a two-hour drive. He said, "Promise me that you will save me a dance before you leave," to which Anne said, "Absolutely." He then went on to say that he would love to get together and asked whether Anne would be open to having drinks or dinner or something. Anne explained that she was going to Dallas the following week to perform with Marvin Hamlisch again, but after that she would be home and yes, she would love to get together.

Anne says that one of the first things she fell in love with was that when he took out his phone to take her number, being in his fifties, he was having trouble seeing the phone and was squinting trying to put her number in. She found it adorable.

He took her phone number, and as he tells it, he didn't know whether she was giving him the right number or not. But he gave Anne his phone number and asked her to let him know that she had arrived safely home when she got home that evening.

They did have a dance, had a little more conversation, and then Anne said goodnight and drove home. By the time Anne arrived at home, there was a text from him saying, "Just wanted to make sure you got home safely," to which she texted back saying, "Yes, I did. Thank you for checking."

The following week, when she arrived in Dallas for her concert, there was a large bouquet of flowers waiting for her in her dressing room. He had looked up Marvin Hamlisch's concert schedule and found out where she would be performing.

From his point of view, the reason he had been at the concert that evening was that the CEO of Johnson & Johnson was on the board of the university where he worked, so he had been there to support him. He had come without a date (the woman walking with him had nothing to do with him, she just happened to be there at the same time), he was sitting at a table with his board members and their spouses, and he was saying, "I really would love to meet this girl." The people at his table said, "Well, what are you going to do? Are you just going to walk up there?" And he said, "Yeah, I've got one shot, to just walk up there and say something. Otherwise, what am I going to do? Email her later and say, 'I was sitting in Row G, Seat 5, did you notice me?'"

So he took a shot, and Anne thought it was very interesting because she had quit dating, and she remembered a friend had said to her years before, when she was still online dating, "Anne, you're not going to meet someone online. You're going to be like in the line at Starbucks. That's how you're going to meet someone. It's going to be something completely random."

And her friend was right. Anne wasn't even going to go to this thing, and there he was.

The week after Anne got back from Dallas, they had their first date, a dinner at the Bedford Post Inn, and it was magical.

It was definitely different than any of the dates she had had, and Anne remembers telling her girlfriends, "This one feels different."

In retrospect, Anne is grateful that she had all the experiences of dating men who were not quite right so she could tell the difference.

Anne and Don were married a year and a half after their first meeting.

All because she said yes to something she would have said no to, and because he had the desire and the guts to risk embarrassment and rejection and go after what he wanted.

I will NEVER Marry Another Actor

Marsha, an actress previously married to an actor who, as she put it, was "the poster child for why you don't want to marry an actor," had made a deal with a friend that if he took the acting class she was leading, she would take the acting class he was leading.

The first day of class, Marsha was clear that the last thing she was looking to find was a date in a theater full of actors. She had been married to one egomaniacal actor, and was not about to make that mistake again!

The class was great, and Marsha did notice one actor she thought was the cutest guy in the room. But that observation was purely aesthetic, since she was not looking for a hookup.

She would later find out that John (the cute guy) had thought she was a cute little Jewish girl. She was, in fact, a cute little Spanish girl, but "two out of three ain't bad."

At the time, Marsha and her best friend, who was also taking the acting class, were planning her best friend's wedding. Every moment they weren't in class, they were huddled in a corner talking invitations, flowers, dresses, etc.

Repeatedly, John would graciously approach them during their "secret meetings" with invitations to coffee, to dinner, to his house for spaghetti—but Marsha was so "out of it," she never realized that these might be invitations for dates, since he was an actor and she did not date actors!

Simultaneously, John was going through a divorce. Marsha had "been there, done that," so she had empathy for his pain, but an actor in the middle of a divorce certainly raised multiple red flags. Marsha was not interested!

Several weeks into the class, John invited Marsha to see him in a play. They'd had some heartfelt talks about his breakup, and she knew he was a lovely guy in need of support, so as a "friend from class," she agreed to go see him in his show.

After the show, Marsha, as a fellow "actor friend" waited to say hello, share her comments on the play and on his acting (the play was strange, he was good), and make her getaway.

All that went out the window when John asked Marsha if he could kiss her. Her first thought was, "Are we on a date?" followed by her saying, "Yes, that would be nice." The kiss was lovely, so when John invited her to go out for a drink, she followed him to the parking lot where they got into their cars to make their way to a restaurant.

As Marsha pulled her car up behind John's truck, more red flags flashed. The truck, which somehow said "irresponsible redneck actor" to her, had North Carolina license plates, the state from which her "practice husband" had hailed, and a dog popped up in the back seat. Marsha thought, "The only thing missing is a gun rack. Who is this guy?"

Fighting every instinct to run, Marsha ended up spending three hours talking and laughing with John in a quiet bar. Making her way back to her apartment that night, after a couple more juicy kisses by her car, Marsha thought, "I am in so much trouble."

They had their first official date the following Tuesday. John took her to see her first Cirque du Soleil, and as Marsha says, "It was a magical beginning that continues to mystify and delight me as we approach our 25th wedding anniversary later this year."

She knew she would never marry another actor. So much for that!

The Play's the Thing

Elyse had enrolled at Queen's College and was taking her first drama class. One of the requirements of the class was that everyone had to go to see whatever play was going on at the college at the time. Elyse went to the show and felt that it was a basic college production, not particularly thrilling, but there was this one actor, Joel, who she thought was amazing and truly stole the show.

When the play was over and everyone was going over to the actors to tell them how wonderful they were, Elyse noticed that Joel, the actor who she really thought was fantastic, was nowhere to be found. Deciding to leave, Elyse was surprised to see him standing outside the theater, all by himself, smoking a cigarette. It struck her as unusual that someone who had just done such a great performance didn't seem interested in sticking around to receive the praise. Too shy to go up and talk to him (possibly because she had kind of a crush on him), Elyse went to her car and drove home.

Fast forward: Elyse decided to join the drama department and started doing their classes and productions. It was a very small department and a lot of the same people were cast over and over again, so Elyse gradually started becoming friends with all of Joel's friends.

Oddly enough, Joel and Elyse hadn't yet spoken to each other, but they were both cast in the play Little Murders, Joel as Elyse's father (it was, after all, a college production) and Joel's current longtime girlfriend as Elyse's mother!

There was definitely a chemistry between Joel and Elyse, but between Elyse's shyness and the fact that Joel's girlfriend was playing her mother, it went unexpressed. It did come out in the fact that when the play required Joel to have some fatherly flirtatious physical business with Elyse, he seemed unable to bring himself to do it. The director, who probably could see the sparks between them better than they could allow themselves to, playfully said, "You're her father. Flirt with her!"

Throughout the whole rehearsal process, Elyse remembers that everyone was extremely friendly and talkative, except Joel. He was all business and never talked to her outside of their scene work together. "OK," she thought. "He hates me."

As time went on and Joel and Elyse were cast in more shows together, they got friendlier and started hanging out more and more. But since Joel's girlfriend was always on the scene (and by the way, Elyse thought she was an amazing actress and admired her greatly) and since Elyse also had a long-term boyfriend at the time, they seemed destined to remain nothing more than colleagues and friends.

As fate would have it, they got cast in a production of Our Town, Elyse as Emily and Joel as George. Elyse remembers that when she was reading the script, she saw there was a kiss in the wedding scene. She panicked. Aware that she had a crush on Joel, she really didn't want to do it. She even went to the director and asked, "Do we have to do the kiss?" (Stupid question, considering it was a wedding scene.) The director said, "Yes, you have to do the kiss." "Well do we have to do it in rehearsal, or can we just do it in the play?" "You have to do it in rehearsal." (By the way, this was the same director who had directed them in Little Murders. Perhaps she knew something they didn't.)

Right before they started rehearsing, Elyse was having a lot of issues with her boyfriend. He was already out of college and not at all involved in or interested in her theater life.

Joel chimed in at this point that the reason he had been so standoffish with Elyse was because his girlfriend, also noticing their chemistry, did not "allow" him to talk to her. There was definitely an undeniable "thing" between Joel and Elyse, and since they were both spoken for, they were, on some level, trying to behave and do the right thing.

Joel and Elyse put off actually doing the kiss in rehearsal for as long as possible, which only served to make it even more of a big deal. When they finally did kiss, Elyse thought, "Oh, this is bad. We're in trouble now."

Being actors on stage gave both of them permission to safely give in to their emotions, and the sixteen times they got married during the run of the show, in a big beautiful theater in front of all those people, became less and less about acting and more and more about their true feelings for each other.

As they look back, they realize that one of the other important turning points for them was the specific play they were doing. Our Town is a brutal and moving play that truly exhorts us to enjoy and make the most of every moment of our lives. Elyse began to realize that being with a boyfriend who was not only not interested in her artistic life but actually resentful of it was not what she wanted in a relationship. And Joel began to realize that although his girlfriend was a wonderful and talented person, their relationship was often filled with conflict and jealousy and disagreement. They had both tried to pretend that they were getting what they wanted, but having who they wanted right there in front of them, doing a wedding scene with them in this particular play, truly opened their eyes.

Elyse broke up with her boyfriend during the run of the show. Even though nothing had come to pass, everyone around Joel and Elyse could see that there was something between them. As word got back to Joel's girlfriend (who had graduated from college), they decided to sit down and discuss it. To his girlfriend's great dismay, they broke up at that meeting.

Joel and Elyse have been together for nine years, and they're both clear that they now have, in actuality, the kind of relationship they had tried to convince themselves they had with their previous partners, but didn't. They never fight, they never bicker, and they work together constantly, in films and in the theater company they started together. They're still not married, but with sixteen onstage weddings under their belt, they might as well be.

"Lamp Man"

It is Monday, October 2, 1978. As Nick waits for a flight to Pittsburgh, he watches Bucky Dent break the hearts of thousands of Boston baseball fans. Nick is on his way to play Lennie in Of Mice and Men at the Pittsburgh Public Theatre. The actor playing George is already in Pittsburgh because he is in the current production. The rest of the cast will arrive in a week, and in the meantime they will have a week to work on the Lennie–George scenes: "Where we going, George?" "Tell me about the rabbits, George." Etc.

Of Mice and Men has exactly one female character, Curly's Wife, and in this pre-Google era, Nick is waiting for the arrival of the rest of the cast to learn about this actress, Beth McDonald.

The out-of-town actors are being housed in an old Victorian mansion that has been broken up into six apartments, and when Nick learns on Sunday that the newly-arrived Ms. McDonald doesn't have enough light in her basement duplex, he grabs a standing lamp and heads downstairs.

He knocks on the door and says, "Lamp Man!" A remarkably beautiful, curly-haired brunette opens the door, thanks him for the lamp, and offers him some tea. He accepts, and they chat for an hour or so before Nick returns to his apartment.

Two days later, the cast has their first read-through and the theater's photographer is there to take some setup shots and some candids of the cast. He takes exactly two individual candid photos: one of Nick and one of Beth. In Nick's, he is watching Beth read, clearly smitten. In Beth's, she is watching Nick read with evident admiration.

Two days later, Nick moves in to her basement duplex; thirty-nine years later, he still celebrates Lamp Man Day every October 8th.

The Bumpy Road to Love (and the Coincidences That Kept Them on It)

Theresa's Story

Theresa was forty-two years old and had never been married before when she met Michael. They fell in love, and within a year they were living together. Shortly after Theresa and

Michael moved in together, Michael became ill, and after a year and a half of Theresa caring for him, he died.

When Michael died, Theresa hit bottom. Bereft and lonely, she did have a couple of relationships over the next few years, but they were not good. Things just weren't working out. Finally one day she said, "You know what? I'm done. I'm gonna just be single the rest of my life, I don't care, I wasn't meant to be married, that's all there is to it."

At that point in her life, Theresa was doing a lot of dancing. She was a member of a swing dance group, she had a dance partner, and she was going dancing at least three nights a week. Around Thanksgiving, Theresa came down with a sinus infection, so she wasn't going out. The infection lingered, and by December 28th she was going so stir-crazy that she said, "Regardless of how bad I feel, I'm going to give myself one hour out of the house to go dancing."

When Theresa walked into the club, it was about 11 p.m., and a girlfriend of hers was dancing, all alone, on the dance floor. Theresa joined her and the two of them began dancing. It was just Theresa and her friend on the dance floor, when this guy walked up to them and asked if he could join them. To which Theresa said, "Sure."

So the guy started dancing with them, and Theresa noticed he was kind of cute but said to herself, "Forget it. Don't even think about it," and the three of them just danced on.

When the music stopped, the guy introduced himself . . . "Gabe." Theresa introduced herself, and Gabe asked what she did for a living. She answered that she had her own business as a massage therapist, and he said, "Wow, I'm a massage therapist too. I just took the licensing test and am waiting to receive my license."

What a coincidence! Not only does he like to dance, but he's also a massage therapist.

So they hung out, and at the end of the night, when Gabe asked for Theresa's number, Theresa said, "You know, I'm really not interested in dating, I'm happy being single, but I'll give you my card because I'm always looking for massage therapists." Theresa's cards were in her car, so Gabe walked her out to her car, and when they exchanged cards they were both struck by how incredibly similar their cards were. The name of Gabe's business was Total Balance. The name of Theresa's business was Total Balance Life Choice. Their logos were extremely similar. On both cards the words "Total Balance" were one under the other with the "L" of the word "Balance" intersecting the word "Total."

What a coincidence!

So Theresa went on her way thinking, "I hope this guy doesn't get the wrong impression." And of course, he did get the wrong impression. He was smitten with her and kept calling, wanting get together. So Theresa went and played pool with him, and they started casually dating.

By Valentine's Day, Theresa was clear that Gabe was not the right guy for her. Although he had his Massage Therapy license, he was still working at his old job as an auto body repairman. He had three adult kids by his previous marriage, and he had issues with his kids. Theresa felt, "This is not for me," and decided it was time to break up with him.

But it was Valentine's Day and she thought, "I can't break up with him on Valentine's Day. That's just cruel." So she figured she'd wait two weeks and then end the relationship.

On Valentine's Day, Gabe came by to have dinner with Theresa, and handed her a little box. Inside was a very unusual heart-shaped jewelry box. It had alabaster and rhinestones on the top, and Gabe had had it engraved. What was bizarre for Theresa was that she knew this jewelry box. She'd seen it before. So when Gabe went into the bathroom that night, Theresa went into her bedroom and opened a little box of memorabilia that she had from Michael. The box Gabe had given her was the exact same jewelry box that Michael had given her on their first Valentine's Day!

What a coincidence!

So Theresa thought, "Alright, Michael. I don't know what you're trying to tell me here, but I won't break up with him just yet."

The next day Theresa called her good friend Barbara and told her the whole story. Barbara said, "OK, Theresa. For two months I've been listening to you tell me what's wrong with this guy. I think he's a good guy and he's good for you. It's time for you to start looking at what's right about him. 'Cause you're not perfect either. Nobody's perfect."

Another friend pointed out that Theresa was still wearing a ring that Michael had given her. "How are you going to let someone new into your life if you're still wearing Michael's ring?"

The next day, Barbara called Theresa and reminded her, "You survived the worst. If this doesn't work out with Gabe, you'll be alright."

And Theresa thought, "She's right. I am going to be fine. So why not see where this goes."

She and Gabe dated for a while, they worked through some of the issues with Gabe's kids, and after a period of time, Gabe suggested they move in together. As they began discussing it, Gabe said, "You know, you've been pretty nasty to me." And as Theresa stopped to think about it, she realized that she didn't like the way they were resolving some of their issues, because they weren't really resolving them. And Theresa said, "If we're going to do this, we need to get some therapy." Gabe said he was totally against therapy, and Theresa said she didn't feel there was anywhere else for them to go. Theresa was not comfortable continuing the relationship without therapy, and Gabe refused to consider it.

At that point they chose to take a week apart to get some space and perspective on the situation. During that week, Theresa worked on processing the idea of letting Gabe go. She didn't want to give him an ultimatum, but she knew what she wanted and needed and Gabe was refusing to cooperate. Even though they were supposedly taking a week apart, Gabe kept calling Theresa, and when they finally got together at the end of the week, Gabe was still sticking to his guns about not wanting to go to therapy. Since they were at Gabe's place, Theresa said she was going upstairs to get her stuff and leave. At this point Gabe said, "Alright, I'll go to therapy. I didn't go to therapy with my ex-wife, and it might have saved our marriage. I don't want to lose you."

So they went to therapy, worked out some things, and Theresa said, "OK. Let's move in together. But I want you to know up front that what that means for me is that within a year we're going to look at getting married." Gabe said, "Alright, I'm not sure I want to get married," and Theresa said, "Fine. In a year let's look at it, and if you still don't want to get married we'll have to reassess, because I know I want to get married."

So a year went by and they happened to be at the house of the same friend who, over a year ago, had told Theresa to give Gabe a chance. During the course of the conversation,

Theresa's friend brought up the subject of marriage and Gabe said that he hadn't been thinking about it.

On their way home that night, Theresa reminded Gabe of their agreement to look at marriage after a year, and Gabe said, "I'm really nervous about getting married because it's working so well now. I'm afraid to get married because my twenty-two-year marriage failed and ended in divorce." Theresa's response was, "If you don't want to get married, you have to tell me that, because I have a decision to make."

A few weeks later it was Theresa's birthday. Theresa and Gabe went to breakfast and Gabe suggested that they go to the beach. Theresa had wanted to paint the stairs on the outside of her house, so she said, "OK, let's get the painting of the stairs out of the way and then we'll go to the beach." Then Gabe said, "I have to tell you something. I don't have a birthday present for you. I went to the store where I wanted to buy your present and they were on vacation." Theresa was upset but figured, "I'm in my fifties. Let me see if I can be an adult about this." So she said, "OK, let's just go to the house and paint, and then we'll go to the beach."

So they went to the house. Gabe went around back to start painting, and Theresa started doing some work in the garden out front. After a little while, Gabe yelled to her, "I need for you to come back and make sure this is the color you want." Slightly annoyed, Theresa thought, "I know it's the color I want. I picked it out." But she walked to the back, and along the riser of the stairs Gabe had painted, "Will you marry me?"

Theresa began crying so hard she couldn't talk. Gabe was a little confused about what the crying meant, so Theresa picked up the paint brush and wrote, "Yes."

Later that day they went to a deli which was owned by their upstairs tenants who asked, "Did you guys get engaged?" Theresa asked, "How did you know?" to which they responded, "We saw it painted on the stairs!"

Six months later they were married, in a beautiful seaside wedding with all of Gabe's children, friends and family in attendance. After the ceremony and the dinner, everybody danced the night away, just as Theresa and Gabe had on the first night they met.

From Gabe's Point of View

Gabe was fairly new to the area, having been brought there by a relationship that had now ended.

Gabe asked a neighbor what a single guy did for entertainment in the area. The neighbor asked Gabe if he liked to dance, and when Gabe said yes, the neighbor told him about a restaurant in the area that had very good live bands on Friday and Saturday nights. Gabe's neighbor went on to warn him that the place had a reputation for being a "pick-up joint" or "meat market."

Gabe soon got up the nerve to check it out.

The place turned out to be just what he'd hoped for. It was full of people between the ages of thirty-something and sixty-something. Gabe soon became a regular there.

Gabe never expected that this would be the place where he would meet the woman with whom he would spend the rest of his life. But one night, between Christmas and New Year's, he was there and, with the band playing, there were only two women, by themselves, on the dance floor. Gabe was blown away by the way one of them was dancing. Without too much thought, he was on his way out there to ask her if he could dance with her. After the song ended and the next one started, his dance partner's friend disappeared into the crowd, leaving Gabe and Theresa dancing by themselves.

Soon after, the night came to an end, and after exchanging contact info, Theresa and Gabe both left . . . separately. On his way home, Gabe realized that having just followed an impulse to walk out on a dance floor with only two people on it, he could have been very embarrassed if he had been turned down.

What the heck. He'd been brave and he'd had a nice evening. So Gabe took another chance, called Theresa and asked her out to the only other place he frequented in town, the Cue and Brew. It was a club that featured bar food, piped-in rock music, and several pool tables.

Gabe and Theresa started seeing each other regularly, and by Valentine's Day, they were exclusive without really discussing it in any great detail.

For Valentine's Day, Gabe bought Theresa a very nice jewelry box and had it engraved. Theresa invited Gabe over to her house for a home-cooked dinner. She had told him several times that she was not known for her cooking, but she was, in actuality, a very good cook.

It was only months later that Gabe found out that Theresa had been planning to break up with him on Valentine's Day, but "felt bad doing it on a day that celebrated one's love for another".

When Gabe found out, he was floored! Careening between thoughts ranging from "How dare you!" to "What! Did you want to see what I got you for a gift first?" Gabe felt like saying "Screw you!" and walking away from the relationship as fast as he could. Even Theresa's explanation made Gabe's stomach churn. He was embarrassed; He was hurt; He was angry; He felt used. His ego was crushed, and for the longest time, whenever Theresa told her story to someone in his presence, he cringed.

Gabe is now grateful that he didn't act on any of those thoughts and feelings. He stuck with the relationship, and today, Gabe is a very happily married man.

Stars Collide

In 1979, Lucie Arnaz was starring on Broadway in Neil Simon's musical They're Playing Our Song, and Laurence Luckinbill was starring on Broadway in Neil Simon's play Chapter Two. They had never met.

Larry was in the middle of a contentious divorce and was battling for custody of his two young children. Lucie describes her romantic life at the time as "going from one hilarious mishap of a relationship to the next, but at that juncture, feeling a lot like Cinderella at the ball" because of the hit show she was in and all the attention heaped on her that year.

On this particular Thursday, Lucie was meeting a fellow actress for lunch at Joe Allen's Restaurant, a popular Theater District hangout.

As they were finishing up lunch, her friend told her that she was sticking around to meet with Larry Luckinbill, who was going to give her some helpful directorial notes, as she was taking over as Larry's costar in the play Larry was in, a part that had formerly been played by Larry's ex-wife. Lucie's friend filled Lucie in on some of the challenges Larry had been facing in his divorce, and Lucie decided to stay and meet Larry and "cheer him up."

Well she must have done a good job, because at this writing they've been married thirty-six years and are still going strong.

"Coincidence is God's Way of Remaining Anonymous"

Daniel, a student at the American International School in Bangkok, did not enjoy social dancing, so he was not looking forward to the dance that the school's Physical Education Department required that he attend. In an unconscious effort to avoid having to dance, he even forgot his dance shoes that day, but the Physical Education instructor still insisted that he participate. So, reluctantly, Daniel lined up on one side of the gym with all the other boys, and faced the other side of the gym where all the girls were lined up.

The way the dance worked was that the line of boys and the line of girls both walked to the center of the gym, and whoever you found yourself facing became your dance partner. Daniel lined up with the other boys, walked to the center of the floor, looked at the Lisa, the girl standing opposite him, immediately fell in love, and said to himself, "This is the girl I'm going to marry." Daniel was thirteen years old and in ninth grade at the time of the dance.

Although Daniel was very interested in pursuing Lisa, Lisa was much more interested in focusing on a having a ballet career, and as such had no time for boys. After ninth grade, Lisa went off to ballet school at the North Carolina School of the Arts, and Daniel's dad dragged him and the rest of his family off to Australia. (Daniel's father was a petroleum engineer and Lisa's father was with the State Department, so both of them moved around the world a lot growing up.)

Daniel didn't see or hear from Lisa for nearly two years—but he never stopped thinking about her! Then one day, while on a family holiday back in the States (on an exhausting, cross-country road trip visiting family scattered up and down the Atlantic coast), Daniel happened to glance up from a book he had been reading in the car just as they passed a giant billboard that depicted a ballerina in arabesque—it was an ad for North Carolina School of the Arts. He knew that Lisa had gone to some fancy dance school in NC, and that was all he knew. But he figured there couldn't be that many ballet schools in a state represented by Jesse Helms, so he hastily jotted down the phone number as their car sped past the sign. When they finally reached his grandparents' home in Virginia, Daniel called the number from the sign and found somebody who knew Lisa, gave him the number to her dorm, and they reconnected. Daniel often thinks that if he hadn't looked up from his book at that precise moment on that two-thousand-mile road trip, he might never have seen her again!

Fast forward several months later: Daniel ended up going to boarding school in Maui, while Lisa's family moved to Jakarta.

Mailing addresses changed, and in those pre-internet/fax days when international phone calls were beyond the means of adolescents, Lisa and Daniel sadly lost contact with each other yet again.

Another two years passed, but Daniel still thought of Lisa constantly. He even went so far as to take ballet classes so that he could be more conversant with her about her passion for dance in the event they should ever meet again. (Dan admits that he can be a little obsessive.)

Then, his freshman year at Georgetown, he heard a rumor that Lisa had left the San Francisco Ballet—wait a minute, wasn't she just in Jakarta? Or was that just her family? How does one keep track?—and had enrolled in college at Old Dominion University in Norfolk, Virginia. The next day, Daniel called information, got the number for ODU and called. He asked the first person who answered the phone if, out of the twenty-five thousand students they had enrolled there, a girl named Lisa Gillespie was one of them. "Coincidentally," the fellow who answered the phone that day was in charge of the Freshman Honors Program orientation and had just (that very morning) met with Lisa who was one of twenty Freshman Honor Students he had helped "orientate." As it happened, he had dropped her off at her first class, not fifteen minutes prior to Daniel's call. Daniel lied and told him that he was a family member and that it was urgent that he speak to her, so he went back and pulled her out of the classroom and put her on the phone with Daniel. That was two weeks before Thanksgiving weekend. Daniel's family was living in Australia and Lisa's parents were in Indonesia (both places much too far away to fly to and back over the holiday weekend), so he convinced her to come up to DC to spend Thanksgiving with him. The rest is history. They've been happily together for nearly forty years.

So let's see: Bangkok, Jakarta, North Carolina, Australia, Maui, a cross-country road trip, Washington, DC, San Francisco, Norfolk and they still managed to end up together. The traveling has not stopped. Daniel, as the owner of his own successful cosmetics company, makes frequent trips to Africa, London, New York, Tokyo, and any number of other far-flung locations on a regular basis, while Lisa still dances all over the world, in places like Paris, London and locations throughout the US. But no matter where they roam, home for their family is now in Los Angeles.

Six Previous Marriages, A Little White Lie, and a Lousy Apartment

The year was 1992. Kelley, coming out of divorce #2, was dating a man she would later refer to as "Dead Man Walking," and Chuck, coming out of divorce #4, was dating a woman who he later referred to as "The Dump-Finder" because she had found him an absolutely horrendous apartment. With six lousy marriages between them and two subsequent partners with whom they were unhappy, these two could possibly have been voted "least likely to succeed in a committed relationship."

Kelley and Chuck didn't know each other, but they had the same singing teacher, Sam Sakarian. One evening, Chuck and Kelley both found themselves sitting in Cafe La Fortuna, an opera-oriented coffee house on the Upper West Side of New York City. Chuck was sitting at one table with his singing teacher, Sam, and Kelley was at another table with two friends who knew Chuck.

Kelley needed new professional photographs, and her friends told her that in addition to Chuck being a great singer, he was also a great photographer. Kelley walked over to Chuck and made an appointment to have her photograph taken.

When Kelley left the table, Chuck asked Sam, "What's her story?" Sam, knowing full well that Kelley was in a relationship, and also knowing full well that it was a horrible relationship, said "She's available!" What Chuck heard in his tone of voice was, "Go get her and save her!"

Chuck took Kelley's head shots and the two of them hit it off. In the course of their conversation, Chuck told her that he was living in a dumpy apartment that his girlfriend had found for him because she wasn't ready to have him move in. Kelley volunteered that she was going to California to visit her father, and Chuck was more than welcome to use her apartment while she was gone.

Chuck never left! Although they hadn't even so much as kissed up to this point, something clicked and Chuck stayed. They waited seven years to get married because Chuck didn't want to saddle Kelley with an IRS debt until he could clear it, which he finally was able to do several years later. They got married on his birthday, because Chuck said he didn't want to have to remember another anniversary. The real reason was that Kelley needed to be married to him for a year in order to be eligible for his Equity Pension before he turned sixty-five.

They've been together for twenty-five years now, in one of the happiest and most committed relationships you will ever see.

A Pair of Panties is the Reason They're Married Today

Carolyn was living in Los Angeles. Kami was living in Indiana. They did not know each other.

One day, Kami returned home after a trip and found a pair of panties that didn't belong to her in her couch. Taking this as undeniable proof that her boyfriend was cheating on her (which he tried to deny, but yes he was), Kami decided to pack up everything and move to L.A. Kami got a job in a bar because a friend of hers from Indiana who was now also in L.A. was a regular customer there and recommended Kami for the job. Carolyn also worked at the same bar, and Kami and Carolyn hit it off and became fast friends.

Kami was living with a roommate she had found on Craigslist, and a short time after they moved in they had a dinner party. At that dinner party, Carolyn met a friend of Kami's roommate named Carlo, who Kami's roommate knew because they were on a soccer team together. Carlo suggested that the next time they all get together they should play Trivia, and he offered to bring his friend Arbi, because Arbi was really smart.

Carolyn found Arbi not only smart, but funny and charming. About two months after they first met, they each decided, coincidentally, to dress as Freddy Mercury for Halloween. That was the beginning of the ongoing relationship that Carolyn calls "without a doubt, the best thing in my life."

So . . . if Kami had not found an unidentified pair of panties in her couch, accused her boyfriend of cheating and found out that he actually had cheated, decided to pick up and move to L.A., had a friend from Indiana who got her a job in a bar where Carolyn worked, befriended Carolyn, invited Carolyn to dinner where she met Kami's roommate (who she'd found on Craigslist), been introduced to Kami's roommate's friend Carlo who suggested they play Trivia and brought Arbi, with whom she immediately hit it off, she would not be married today.

Amazing the way the universe works.

Sue & Kenro

Sue was interviewing to be the president's assistant at Japan Travel Bureau. As she was waiting, she saw this tall (unusual for a Japanese man), dark, and very handsome man pass behind the receptionist and remembers thinking, "Wow! He's tall and really, really handsome. I hope I get this job!"

Well, she did get the job and started two weeks later, but this mystery man was nowhere to be found. Sue assumed he might have been a manager visiting from Japan, so she just let it go and focused on her new job.

Two weeks after she started work, Sue turned around in the coffee room and ran right into him. With a flustered energy that said, "Oh I know you but I haven't met you but I'm already crushin' on you," she introduced herself to him, told him she was the president's new assistant, kind of bowed to him and scooted out of the room.

(Later, Kenro told Sue that his first impression of her was, "Pretty eyes and nice big tits!")

Charming!

Two weeks later, at the annual holiday party, Sue discovered that part of the reason she was hired to be the president's assistant was because the president was fascinated by her dance background (which was only mentioned on her resume as "other interests"). All of a sudden, her boss became John Travolta, dragging Sue onto the dance floor so he could show off his moves. She was horrified. She was wearing an electric blue accordion pleated dress that flew out in all directions as he spun her (thank goodness she always wore a half-slip), so she spent her time on the dance floor trying to keep her dress down.

Oy!

This little incident led to ten short, drunk, white-socked Japanese men, many of whom had their work ties now tied around their foreheads, eagerly asking her to dance . . . maybe because their noses ended up being right smack in her cleavage (Sue is 5'9" in high heels). If she learned anything that night about working in this Japanese company, she learned that liquor was not a friend to these otherwise sweet and docile Japanese business men. They had this thing where you were pretty much allowed to act like an ass if you apologized for it the next day.

Well, she was done. She'd had enough. She looked over at Kenro, this tall drink of water, went over to him and asked him to dance. A first in her lifetime. It was a slow song, because as Sue later said, "Mama was no fool!"

She swears that in that moment, in his arms, she knew she was going to marry him. Not only did the 3.5 children and the wood-paneled station wagon float by in her mind, but she felt safe in his arms and just "knew." She had never been attracted to any Asian man before, but her "type" was tall, dark, handsome, and a bit of a bad boy (which he was, especially in the Japanese community) and she was hooked.

Shortly thereafter, they met up in an art gallery on their lunch hour and when they realized they shared that interest, they started to date as friends. A year later they were a couple, dating secretly (very sexy—no one in the company knew, not even Sue's Assistant.) The next year, Sue left the company and they moved in together. They lived together for four years, and one day Kenro came home from a tour to Switzerland (a place they mine diamonds) with what looked like a black velvet necklace box and handed it to her. She was disappointed and remembers thinking, "Crap, he only got me a diamond necklace."

(What a brat!)

But, bouncing all over the inside was a gorgeous diamond ring. His proposal was, "You're not going to make me get down on my knee are you?"

Again, how romantic!

But Sue didn't care. Kenro had proposed. And Sue said, "Yes."

On Tuesday, March 21, 1988, they woke up and Kenro said, "Let's do it!" To which Sue replied, "We don't have time...we have to get to work." He then said, "No stupid, let's get married today!" They did.

At this writing they have been married twenty-eight years, having lived together for four years before that. Sue says that honestly she cannot remember her life before Kenro.

After Great Loss Comes Great Love

Pete Before Tracey

As Pete describes it, he had lived most of his life up to 2007 in "blissful ignorance," having never really suffered loss or hardship of any kind. Pete had grown up in a happy home, married the love of his life, and had two great kids.

The second Saturday in August of 2007 started very much like any other. Pete and his wife Colleen were just waking up and planning their day when she paused, grabbed his hand, and asked if he felt a lump on her breast. From there, their lives spiraled into the dark and tragic world of cancer. She fought a valiant fight for two and a half years, finally succumbing on January 14, 2010.

Pete felt empty, depressed and heartbroken. Yet somehow he knew that however shattered his world was, the real world would continue on and at some point, if he did not get back on track, he would be left behind . . . another victim.

Life slowly morphed into his "new normal." There were a few amazing friends who knew him well enough to give him his space, but also to push and prod him along his healing road.

Then one day in the late summer of 2011, Pete realized something that hit him like a ton of bricks. He was no longer lonely for Colleen. He was just lonely. It sounds like a small thing, but it was a huge moment. He was ready to join the world.

Pete had learned from experience that communication is the key to everything. When Colleen was near the end, they'd had had a heart-wrenching talk in which they bared their souls to each other. Colleen told Pete that she wanted him to find someone else someday. She wanted him to be happy. It was one of the most selfless things Pete had ever experienced.

Although Pete was basically a shy person who rarely initiated social contact, he took a deep breath and put himself out there on match.com.

He posted the following long-winded but honest message:

I have heard some unbelievable stories from female friends about some of the guys out there and the stuff they try to pull. That really isn't me at all. I'm not looking for a hookup, but am hoping to meet someone who wants to start a relationship. I have been out of the dating scene for a while, but it must be like riding a bicycle, right? Well, maybe it's a bit more intricate than that. Have the rules changed a lot in the past eleven years?

I am the lucky dad of two great children. I love them with all my heart and I am raising them to the best of my ability. They are 6 and 8 and are amazingly grounded and have seen great sorrow, but luckily, greater joy in their lives. We have bonded into quite a team over the past couple of years and I am constantly amazed at how wonderful they are.

I have worked in Boston TV news for over fifteen years, but am embarking on a big change. My love of history has always brought me pleasure, but now I am making the leap to become a high school history teacher. Summers off sounds pretty cool . . . right?

My favorite hobby has been being a restoration volunteer on the USS Massachusetts in Fall River, MA. It has been a seventeen-year love affair where I get to bang metal, scrape paint and meet members of the Greatest Generation and do something to preserve such an important part of our history.

I would describe myself as a good and caring person with old fashioned values. Being able to laugh has helped through some really tough times in the past few years.

I am a fairly simple person and am not really into hitting clubs but have also found that some of the best times are when you go outside your comfort zone . . . and so here I am on Match.

I have been lucky enough to travel quite a bit, but since my kids are small, it's been Disney for the past few years. I want to take them to Ireland, Italy (I have never been) and some day drive across country as I did with my folks when I was a kid. (It was a lot like the Chevy Chase movie . . . without Christy Brinkley.)

If you are sure of yourself but also like to have the door held for you, we'll get along just fine.

Thanks for reading. I hope to hear from you soon.

Under his details, Pete put:

> Relationship: Widower
> Have kids: Yes, and they live at home (2)
> Want kids: Probably not
> Ethnicity: White/Caucasian
> Body Type: Slender
> Height: 5'9"
> Faith: Christian/Catholic
> Smoke: No Way
> Drink: Never

Even with all the details about his wholesome family life and his desire for a serious, committed relationship, Pete was quickly contacted by someone looking for "grown-up fun" and by another woman offering to come right over and "get down to business." Pete told her he was reading to his kids and that might not work.

He was about to give up when he received a message from Tracey.

Tracey Before Pete

Tracey had recently come out of a failed marriage and a tragedy of her own. Married at the age of twenty-eight, Tracey had immediately gotten pregnant. Her son was born prematurely and with extremely serious medical problems. Tracey's whole life changed as she spent most of her time at the hospital caring for her desperately ill son. Several months after his birth, Tracey's son died.

After her son's death, Tracey tried valiantly to keep her marriage together. But as often happens in such cases, the intense grief, the anger, the confusion and the inability to cope with the tragedy as a couple caused the marriage to deteriorate and finally end.

The one good thing that came out of the marriage was the birth of a beautiful, healthy daughter.

With the marriage over, Tracey began the process of rebuilding her life as a single parent.

After a while, Tracey realized that she was content. In fact, she was happy. She had a wonderful daughter, a great family, and a busy, fulfilling work life. She had no interest in looking for another relationship.

One day she was having a conversation with her uncle, and he said, "Tracey, it's time to get back out there!" "What do you mean, back out there?" was Tracey's reply.

"It's time to start dating."

Tracey told him, "I wouldn't even know where to begin looking," to which he replied, "On match.com of course." Everyone does it!"

Reluctantly and with trepidation, Tracey placed an ad on match.com. It read:

> I am hoping to find someone to have a simple, happy relationship with. As someone who has gone through a divorce recently, I am new to dating (again). It seems totally weird to be doing this . . . but I am an optimist am hoping to find someone special.

As had happened to Pete, Tracey was immediately bombarded by people looking for hookups, including people sending pictures of body parts she had no desire to see. One email in particular stands out in her memory. It was from somebody more than twenty years older than she, and it read:

"Princess! You are magnificent! A beautiful woman should always be celebrated, kitten! Jim"

Ugh!

Tracey was about to give up and close her account when she noticed that there was a feature on match.com where the website suggested compatible matches for you. She decided to give it one more try.

The first one she came across was Pete's. She liked what he said and liked the picture, so she wrote back.

Tracey and Pete

Pete received Tracey's message and immediately responded. From the get-go it was clear that they had a connection. Not only did they have mutual interests and mutual desires for a particular kind of relationship, but because they had both been through great heartache and loss, they were able to empathize with each other's experience. Tracey was perfectly comfortable with the fact that Pete had truly loved his first wife, and had no problem with his talking about her as much as he needed to. Pete could understand the pain that Tracey had been through in losing a child, and was supportive whenever Tracey needed to talk about it.

In short order they decided they should meet. From the moment they sat down in a restaurant for their first date, the stars seemed to align and they became inseparable.

They are now happily married, a combined family with three children and three sets of grandparents nearby.

They are both clear that the early challenges and losses they went through have made them appreciate the sweetness of every moment they are together. They never take it for granted.

He Used the Right Word

It was 1999, and Jane, an extremely intelligent and successful forty-year-old banker and financial consultant (and a great singer as well—that's how I first met her), had just started a new marketing and communications consulting business and was feeling annoyed because it was a hot August Sunday and she had to work. So she was sitting in her apartment at her desk working on whatever she was working on, distracting herself by surfing around the Internet. In the course of her surfing she came across love@aol.com and, on a whim, decided to post an ad for herself. These being the very early days of Internet dating, she had no idea what might happen, but what the heck! She was bored.

By the next morning she had forty-five responses. For the next few months, Jane went on a dating spree, meeting some very nice men, but no one special enough. Jane's girlfriends were in a panic because since online dating was so new, they were worried for her safety. So they developed a code—whenever Jane went out on a date she had to call one of them to tell them where she was and what she was doing.

Jane was actually dating another guy when she saw David's ad, which was titled "Music and Intelligence." Intrigued, she responded to it. They spent a little time talking on the phone, and when David used the word "derivative" in a sentence and was not referring to anything in the financial markets, Jane knew she had found someone special.

They decided to meet on a Saturday afternoon at the Starbucks at the corner of 67th and Columbus in Manhattan. It was the longest first date in history. They had coffee, walked up to the Metropolitan Museum of Art, had lunch with a friend of Jane's, and David didn't leave until after midnight.

So the die was cast, but what was really funny about the whole thing is that David was from the next town over from where Jane grew up in New Jersey, Jane's mother had taught school in that town, and although she'd never had David for a student, David's mother and Jane's mother had friends in common, so Jane was able to check him out pretty easily. But the fact is that once they met they were never really apart.

The Bartender Had His Eyes Open

On Memorial Day weekend in 1990, Richard was working a crowded late-night shift at Marie's Crisis, a cabaret club in New York's Greenwich Village. At the end of his shift, as Richard was getting ready to go home, the bartender said, "There was a cute guy in here tonight who I think is interested in you!" Richard said, "Why didn't you tell me?" and the bartender told Richard that he'd told the guy to come back Monday night since, it being the end of the holiday weekend, they probably wouldn't be terribly busy.

When Richard arrived at the club for his Monday night shift, Danny was already sitting at the end of the bar. Richard introduced himself and found out that Danny was indeed the guy that the bartender had referred to.

Danny stayed for Richard's entire shift ('til 4 a.m.!) and Richard asked him if he would like to go to breakfast. They went over to the Sheridan Diner and sat and talked 'til 7 a.m. Danny told Richard he was going uptown, and if Richard was too, Danny could drop him off, as Danny lived in a suburb north of the city and was driving home.

When they got to Richard's place, Richard told him that if he wanted to crash for a few hours (no funny business) before making the long drive home, he was welcome to do so.

They crashed, and Danny left at 1 p.m. with the promise that they would get together soon.

Just after Danny left, Richard got a call from a friend who offered him free tickets to a show. Richard called Danny and left a message on his answering service asking if he would like to go. Danny called back and said yes, and they went on their first date.

That was twenty-six years ago, and Richard and Danny have been together ever since. Richard says that he wasn't looking for a "partner" when Danny came into his life, but the moment he met him, he knew Danny was his soulmate.

Let's Get You Out of Those Wet Clothes

Roger Anthony Yolanda Mapes, who refers to himself as a "non-binary transgendered person," was going by the name Yolanda when he and Glen met at a Thanksgiving party held by one of their mutual friends. They had seen each other around town several times, but had never really connected. They had both given up on finding a relationship because of past failures.

The day of the Thanksgiving party it was pouring rain, and Glen arrived at the party soaking wet. Yolanda had not yet arrived. The host suggested that Glen put his clothes in the drier and go sit on the landing while his clothes dried. Glen was sitting in his underwear when Yolanda came up the stairs. Their eyes locked and they were immediately attracted to each other. Yolanda said, "Hi," Glen said "Hi," they immediately started kissing, and that was that.

They had to work out some kinks along the way, but that original kiss led to their eleven-year relationship and their marriage in 2011.

They're still going strong, and they weren't even looking for it.

I asked Yolanda if he had ever had a conversation with Glen before their meeting on the stairs, and Yolanda said:

"Glen would come to my concerts but I wasn't aware of him. If he introduced himself to me, I don't remember. However we both were members of a group called the Radical Faeries that met for heart circles at the LGBT Center. I remember him at one of those circles and thought he was cute but didn't pursue it.

"There was something magical about that Thanksgiving Day when we finally connected. It was as if the universe had been preparing us to really drop the walls that we had built around the possibility of a true loving relationship. Before the party we did know each other but didn't really see each other. On that landing in the stairwell, when we looked into each other's eyes, there was the recognition of our oneness with each other. It surprised both of us!"

Come Fly with Me

As a single mom, Sandi found herself in the unusual yet rather appropriate position of running a singles' tennis business. A very nice married woman, who had a husband who traveled a lot, would attend Sandi's singles tennis parties. One day this woman came to Sandi and said, "I have a friend I think you should meet." Sandi said, "Thank you, but not right now. I'm seeing someone."

Well, as Sandi put it, "Time passes, and so do boyfriends," so a few months later Sandi mentioned to this woman that if her friend would like to call her, she was free. And sure enough, a couple of days later, Sandi received a call from Bob Durell—Robert Durell, MD—and he said, "Would you like to go flying?"

Having not even met the man (although he came from a fine source), Sandi, being an "old fashioned kinda gal," felt it was best to keep her feet on the ground and meet him for a more normal date so they could get to know one another.

They had a lovely first date walking the grounds of an arboretum, talking, lunching on hot dogs, and learning about each other. Bob was flying single engine planes at the time (the impetus for Sandi to start flying lessons—which she later did) and when he called a couple of days later and said, "Now would you like to go flying?" Sandi, with a bit of trepidation, said "Yes." And he said, "Of course, bring your daughter," as he thought she'd enjoy the experience. Sandi's daughter was a young child at the time, but Sandi brought her along.

Their trip took them to Block Island, where they had a lovely day meandering about and having lunch, and before they knew it, finding it was time to return back to Long Island.

And so it went: flying to Hyannis; several more trips to Block Island and other destinations; dates in New York . . . and within a year they were Dr. and Mrs. Robert Durell.

One thing that had given Sandi second thoughts about Bob was that she was his third wife. But the third time turned out to be a charm, and thirty-six years later, they are still happily together. None of which would have happened, had it not been for her unique singles' tennis business, and the married woman who serendipitously attended her parties and introduced them.

Never Talk to Strangers (or You Might Meet the Love of Your Life)

Judy was twenty-one years old, working at Saks Fifth Avenue in New York, enjoying the young, single life, and casually dating about five different guys with no thoughts of getting married in the near future.

It was a beautiful spring night in April at about 9 p.m. Judy had worked late and was now standing on the subway platform at 51st Street and Lexington Avenue, waiting for the train to take her uptown.

Out of the corner of her eye, Judy noticed a gorgeous hunk of a guy about two car-lengths down the platform, but all of a sudden her attention was diverted by a blood-curdling scream from across the way, on the other side of the tracks.

The subway came, Judy got on, and as she stood holding onto the train strap, she realized that the handsome hunk she had spotted on the platform was standing right next to her. Clearly he had followed her.

So here they were, standing side by side, electricity flying between them, but not saying a word to each other. The subway stops passed; 59th Street, 68th Street, and at 77th Street Judy got off the train.

As Judy got to the top of the stairs, she did a little pivot of her head to see if the guy was following her. Not seeing him anywhere, she proceeded to walk uptown.

Two blocks later, Judy was waiting for a red light to change when she felt a little tap on her shoulder, and there he was!

He told Judy, "I would love to meet you. I've never done this before. I've gotten off a stop early to meet you. Could I buy you a drink?"

Judy looked at him and thought, "Wait a minute here! I was born and raised that you don't talk to strangers, but this guy is just too exciting."

Trying to make some conversation that would buy her a little time to get a bead on who this guy was, Judy said, "Do you know what happened to Martin Luther King?" And he said, "No, I haven't heard." Judy told him, "He was shot." At that point she realized that that was probably what the blood-curdling scream across the subway platform was. Someone must have just heard the news.

Then Judy said to him, "I'm on my way to a political meeting. If you want to come with me, maybe we can go out afterward." He did come, there were about a hundred people there, they stayed for an hour or so, and having survived the meeting, they decided to go out.

He took her to a place called "And Vinnie's," which was a couple's spot. You couldn't get in unless you were a couple. They sat and talked at the piano bar, and after getting each other's life stories, they spent the evening dancing, and had an altogether wonderful time.

That was April.

Judy and Carl were married the following November and enjoyed a long and happy life together, sharing their love of dancing, theater, cabaret and jazz, tennis, golf (he taught her how to play), their mutual career interests (she was in fashion, he was in advertising), and their sense of humor.

They were married forty-four years when Carl passed away in 2013.

Snap Decisions

Debbie, an actress who lived in London, was on tour with a theater company in Germany. She had a two-week holiday coming up, and she decided she wanted to go somewhere else in the world rather than heading home to the UK or staying on in Germany.

Debbie's sister, who lived in Sydney, Australia said, "Come on over and visit me for two weeks." Debbie's friends thought it was a really bad idea, because it's such a long flight and she was already tired from touring. Even to Debbie, the trip didn't make any sense, except for the fact that she really wanted to go. Her friends suggested that Debbie wait until the tour was over and then go to Australia for a longer period of time, but Debbie knew that as soon as her tour ended she would be hungry to look for her next acting job.

Debbie had a boyfriend at the time, but the relationship was straining under the stress of not seeing each other because of the tour. She thought he could come to Australia with her and that way they could spend some time together, but he broke up with her just before they were due to go.

Debbie was a bit sad about the breakup, but not completely heartbroken. Deep down, she knew that the end of that relationship had been in the cards.

So off she flew to Sydney to spend some time with her sister and her family. When Debbie got there, her sister mentioned that she'd bought a table at the races. Debbie thought it would be fun. She'd get to dress up and bet on the horses.

Debbie was sitting at her table at the Derby Day Races when she looked up and saw a man walking by. He looked at her and smiled, she smiled back, and he walked on.

She had lousy luck on the horses all day, so she decided to bet on a horse named Blue Murder, who was running in a race in Melbourne. It was one of the televised races they were showing in between the live races in Sydney. And lo and behold, her horse won! Debbie went up to collect her winnings, and out of nowhere the man who had smiled at her earlier came up and started chatting with her. She told him she was only in Sydney for one more week, and he asked if he could have her telephone number; perhaps they could go for a drink and a bite to eat. Debbie said, "Fine," but this being before the age of cell phones, and it having been a long while since she'd been chatted up by a stranger, there was a bit of an awkward shuffle as Debbie tried to remember her sister's phone number and find a pen and paper to write it down.

They finally got it sorted out, said their goodbyes, and Debbie continued to the counter to collect her winnings . . . only to discover she'd written her number on the back of her only winning ticket!

Debbie and Brett had their first date, and it wasn't until he was dropping her back at her sister's house that she realized that she hadn't looked at the time once. They'd spent about five hours together yet there still seemed to be so much more to say.

After Debbie's last week in Sydney was up, they parted and kept in contact long-distance. When Debbie's tour finished, she went back to Sydney and they started dating. They moved in together six months later and got married two months after that.

Actually, they eloped, and for seven months didn't tell anyone in their family that they were married. (Her family nearly disowned her after that one.)

Three years later, Brett decided to leave his business and asked Debbie what she would do if she could do absolutely anything. Debbie said, "I'd move back to London." Brett said, "OK, let's do it!" Three weeks later, they'd sold everything and bought a one-way ticket.

Last year, fifteen years after they were married, they made a similar "snap" decision. They sold all their stuff, rented out their London apartment, and now they live as nomads, traveling full time, enjoying the world and their life together.

Sometimes those "snap" decisions are the best decisions.

They Met the "Old Fashioned" Way
(Through Personal Ads)

In the days before the Internet, there were the personal ads.

People would put an ad in the paper, saying what they were looking for, and people who were interested had to write a letter to the paper which was then forwarded to the person who placed the ad, who could choose whether they wanted to write back.

Allen had a friend who was wanting to meet someone but was afraid to place an ad. To support that friend, Allen said that he would place an ad for himself as well.

Allen never looked at or answere any of the responses to his ad, since he had simply placed it to show solidarity with his friend. But a few months later, Allen suddenly realized, "Hey, I'd like to meet someone too!"

At that time, The Advocate, a national gay publication, was one of the only places where gay people could place ads, so Allen wrote an ad and sent it in.

The ad read:

> I have everything I need in my life but I'm seeking someone to share it with. I'm a Taurus.

Allen received quite a few responses with lewd photos, men holding beer bottles, and men just interested in hooking up, but one response, from David, caught his attention.

It was handwritten on a piece of colorful, fanciful stationery, and it said:

> I liked your ad in The Advocate. Simple, knowledge of self, seeks another, caring. I too am looking for someone special. If you're interested, my birth sign is Leo. I just got through writing a succinct description myself which was rather good, just too dull. Not to say that I don't like to be serious, but I'm seeking someone for more than affection, concern, and security. I want someone who can be sharp and hilarious, who can help me play the clown as well as the sage, and play with me. Challenge as well as succor. I'm 30, lived here 6+ years including 5 in the same place and am sensitive but not fragile. Call (phone number): days are good, we'll get a chance to meet. (Not Thursdays.)

> —Dave

Dave says that what he liked about Allen's ad was not only that it was not all about sex, but also that Allen was not seeking someone else to either take care of him or make up for his own deficiencies. Dave was clear that if the person he met was not complete in himself, Dave didn't want the responsibility of making up for what the guy was lacking.

Allen responded to Dave's letter immediately, and the first date they could get together was about a week later, on the afternoon of December 31. They met at a juice bar and talked for a long while, really hitting it off. During the conversation, Dave mentioned that he had a policy of not sleeping with people on the first date. His reason for this was that he felt that if he did, the relationship immediately became a hookup, and he was looking for more than that.

Also, during the course of their chat, they each mentioned that they were invited to New Year's Eve parties that they were not particularly looking forward to attending.

They parted company and greed to get together again soon.

On the bus ride home, Allen began thinking to himself; "I really like this guy. I'm not interested in going to my New Year's Eve party, and neither is he. I'm going to call him and invite him over to my house for New Year's Eve." Allen called Dave and Dave reminded him of his commitment to not sleep with anyone on the first date. Allen understood, but he told Dave that he felt it was important to ask for what he wanted. Dave agreed to come over for the evening, he ended up sleeping over, and the relationship began.

About four months later, Dave was going over a list he'd made some time before of qualities he wanted in a relationship. Although Allen had many of those qualities, there were other places where Dave was not entirely sure he was satisfied.

Dave felt it was time to reassess and decide whether he really wanted to continue with this relationship.

In reassessing, Dave came to the conclusion that he needed to stay and give it more time to see where it would go.

Dave jokingly says that he's still doing that. It's been thirty-seven years.

Note: In his letter to Allen, Dave said he wanted someone who can be "sharp and hilarious." After a long and successful career as a set designer for television and theater, Allen has spent the past several decades as a successful author of dozens of humor books, and is known as the world's only "Jollytologist."

I'll Show You How It's Done!

When Scott was in college, he had a roommate who was very shy. One day, his roommate said to him, "How do you do it? You just seem to have no trouble meeting girls."

Scott's response was, "I'll show you."

They were at a college street fair, so Scott said to his roommate, "Pick out any girl at random, just make sure she's pretty, and I'll show you how I meet her." Scott's roommate pointed to an attractive girl behind one of the tables at the fair, and as it happened she looked up just as she was being pointed to.

Scott walked up to her, and having nothing to say to her since he didn't know her at all, opened with, "Is that a Grateful Dead poster?" She said, "Yes it is," they began to talk, and before they knew it, Scott and Michelle were dating.

A few months later they broke up and went their separate ways.

Five years later, Scott was watching CBS News and he saw a report about a PETA "I'd rather go naked than wear fur" demonstration, and there was Michelle standing in public in a pink towel. He switched to NBC and there she was again. ABC also ran a story on the demonstration, and once again, Michelle was on the screen. Scott hadn't seen her in five years, but he thought, "I should let her mother know that she's on TV?" So he called Michelle's mother who said, "Yes, I know. Michelle is at home."

They're married today.

Paying for It

When asked how he met his wife, Steve replied: "I went out on a blind date forty-eight years ago, and I've been paying for it ever since!"

AUTHOR'S NOTE: When I first was told this story, I laughed with recognition. Being Jewish and having been born in the Bronx, I could think of so many couples of my grandparents' generation who had long, devoted marriages of fifty or sixty years in which they hardly talked or, when they did talk, bickered constantly. And yet they stayed together. When my editor first read this story, she asked me to take it out, finding it mean-spirited and sexist. Although I agreed with her that it presented a kind of relationship I would never want to have, I found myself strangely reluctant remove it. For some reason, this one-liner story (think of comedian Henny Youngman, who made his career on the one-liner, "Take my wife . . . please") seemed, to me, to not only be a necessary part of presenting the panorama of possible relationships, but also reverberated as a part of my own roots. In exploring why the story was so important to me, I came to a deeper understanding of how each relationship is unique and can have a purpose and meaning to the people in it, even if others might judge it or not understand it

My interest in couples and their stories goes way back. When I was young and first began to entertain the idea that I wanted to be in a long, committed relationship, I looked at longstanding couples to see how they behaved. I expected to find people who went around the house saying, "Oh my darling, I'm so in love with you, you are my life, my love." But what I found, in many cases, was that the conversations were more like, "What are you talking about! You're driving me nuts! Always bothering me with the same thing!"

I knew one couple, the parents of my best friend in high school, who would literally swear at each other and insult and belittle each other in the course of a normal, after-school conversation over cookies and milk. I once asked her, "How do you take this?" to which she answered, "Take what?" I replied, "The abusive language?" Her answer was, "Oh, please. He's just insecure and feels like he needs to talk like that. It goes right over my head." (They stayed devotedly married for over fifty years, and when he became ill, she lovingly nursed him through a stroke and a heart condition.) The wife of one of my mentors, a brash and funny lady who reminded me of Bette Davis, once said to me, "Our marriage is perfect! If only I had my own apartment!"

In looking at relationships for all these years, it's become clear to me that we each get into them to work through things we need to work through, to work out our own childhoods, and to try to be with someone who complements and accepts both our strong points and our flaws. We also usually participate in relationships based on our upbringing, our history, and the "rules" we learned from our own parents. So what some might label sexist or abusive, others with different backgrounds and a different set of "rules" about relationships might find perfectly normal. I think the point is that it's not for us to judge, since we can't know what two people are getting out of a relationship unless we're inside it.

And funnily enough, when I've asked people like Steve why they stay in their marriage if it's so terrible, their response is usually a shocked "Are you kidding? What are you talking about? Why would I leave? I love her."

As the French say, "Chacun à son goût." Each to his own taste.

Sometimes Ya Gotta Take Risks

Over twenty years ago, Emma was living in Cleveland, and she was involved with CILBGO, The Cleveland Irish Lesbian, Bi, Gay Organization, which was working in solidarity with an organization in New York City which was lobbying to allow LGBT people to march in the St. Patrick's Day Parade. (Twenty years later, that did in fact happen.)

Through her work in CILBGO, Emma met a woman named Mary. Emma found Mary attractive but at the time Mary was dating someone else, so Emma and Mary simply worked together as part of the CILBGO organization.

One day, Emma called Mary about something to do with the group, because Mary was the secretary. In the middle of the conversation, Mary started to cry and said, "Today is a really hard day for me because I just broke up with my girlfriend." Emma was empathetic and said, "I'm really sorry to hear that. Of course don't worry about anything to do with the group right now."

But Mary responded, "It's OK. I'm a little upset but I knew it wasn't going to work out, and frankly, I have a list of other people I'd like to date so I'm trying to think positive."

Emma said, "OK. I hope you feel better." and they said goodbye and hung up.

The moment Emma put down the phone she thought, "Wow. She just broke up and she has a list of people she wants to date. I've been admiring her for months. I wonder if I'm on that list."

Emma waited an appropriate number of weeks, and decided to call Mary and tell her how she felt about her. Too afraid to talk to Mary in person, Emma called at a time when she knew Mary would be at work so she could leave a carefully written and rehearsed message on her answering machine.

The message Emma planned to leave was:

"I know you just broke up about a month ago, and I heard you say that you have a list of people you're interested in, and if I'm not currently on the list, I'd like to be added to the list."

Emma dialed the phone.

Mary answered the phone!

Flustered at first, Emma decided, "What the heck!" and told Mary how she felt.

Mary burst into tears and said, "Oh, it's too soon, I just broke up a month ago, I'm not ready to think about this." Emma realized that perhaps Mary had just been trying to sound positive when she had originally said she'd had a list of people she was waiting to date, and that, in fact, it was too soon. Emma decided to just let it go.

Long story short, as a result of that call, which had been extremely awkward and embarrassing for Emma, when Emma and Mary saw each other at a CILBGO demonstration three weeks later, Emma asked Mary if she would like to go and get a cup of coffee. Coffee led to dinner, at which Emma and Mary had a long talk, mostly about politics (which was a turn-on for Mary) and that dinner was the beginning of a long, committed relationship.

Emma and Mary were the first couple to have a civil union in Vermont, and one of the first couples to get married in California.

"Duh!"

Joan and Mark went to the same college, but they didn't know each other. One evening, Joan went to hear a rock band made up of fellow students play at a club. One of the band members was interested in Joan, so he offered to drive her home after the concert in the band van. Mark was also in that van.

Joan and Mark hit it off, so after they'd dropped her off at her apartment and Mark got back to his, Mark called Joan and they ended up talking for over an hour.

It turned out they were in the same speech class and Joan, liking Mark, suggested that instead of doing their individual speech assignments, the two of them play guitars and sing a song together. This entailed their spending some time rehearsing together and getting to know each other better.

After they performed their song in class, Joan said to Mark, "Do you want to go to the Luau party my sorority is having next week?"

To which Mark responded, "I would like to come . . . but I don't have a date."

Duh!

Joan said, "I'm asking you to be my date!"

They went to the party, a week later Mark moved into Joan's apartment with Joan and her roommates, and they've now been married for over forty years.

Twelve Steps to Finding Love

Doug, a longtime member of Alcoholics Anonymous (an organization whose purpose is to help alcoholics become and remain sober), and Gloria, a longtime member of Al-Anon (an organization designed to help people coping with the issues that arise from living with or being raised by an alcoholic), did not know each other.

Gloria was twenty-eight years old. Having been single and enjoying life on her own for four years, Gloria felt that she was ready to begin looking for a new relationship. The dating scene had become overbearing due to men who either had frisky hands, wanted to jump into bed, or wanted to rush into marriage.

Gloria was on a spiritual path as a result of having been in Al-Anon for years, and had begun not only to discover herself, but also to become clearer on the type of man she desired for marriage.

For several years now, Gloria had been attending the annual Al-Anon convention. This year, it was moved to a new town fairly far from her home, so off she went with some trusted lady friends from her home group.

On Saturday evening, Gloria put on a pretty dress, put her hair up in a French twist, and headed out to attend the dance. As she walked out the door of her hotel room, several of her friends greeted her with, "Wow, don't you look very nice!" Her reply was "I'm gonna find me a man!" They all laughed, and off to the dance they went.

Doug was forty-two years old, and after many years of hard drinking and singing in bands, he was now nine years sober. It was strange to him, when he got sober, how very shy he was around women. He was fine in work situations or in the AA rooms, but incredibly awkward at social events.

Doug had met a nurse in his rehab aftercare and had had a quick relationship-wedding-divorce, so he was also a little gun-shy. Since that time, Doug had developed a great circle of friends in AA, and had also developed a fabulous new hobby—scuba diving. Diving all the great wrecks in the North Atlantic was dangerous, exciting, and a physical adventure, and it really helped snap Doug out of his alcoholism.

Doug and his AA friends loved to dance. Whenever they could, they would go to a meeting, go out to dinner, and then go to a sober dance. There weren't so many sober dances at that time, so they thought they would take the opportunity to go to the Al-Anon dance, even though they weren't members of Al-Anon.

Shortly after Gloria arrived at the dance, she became aware that a man she had previously dated was also in attendance. She decided that although it was awkward, she was not going to let that ruin her fun.

At one point, as she walked across the room to get a soda, her eyes fell on the bluest of blue eyes she had ever seen. And they belonged to a handsome man at that. She greeted him with a "Hello," and he replied in turn.

Doug had arrived at the dance, and the first thing he noticed was that the music was loud and there was a big crowd on the dance floor.

Cruising the room, the next thing he noticed was a brunette with her hair in a bun, wearing a sexy, long green skirt with a slit up the side. He was interested.

They passed each other in the crowd several times, each time making lots of eye contact but just murmuring "Hello" and passing each other by.

Eventually, Gloria walked up to Doug and asked him to dance. For Doug, that changed everything. His shyness disappeared. They were now on "his turf," the dance floor. With all his years singing in rock bands, Doug loved to dance, and he was a great dancer.

They danced, tried to talk the best they could over the loud music, and found themselves laughing hard through the conversation. Doug shared with Gloria that he was a member of AA, was nine years sober, and he and his friends had been a bit scared to enter Al-Anon territory as they thought they might be considered "the enemy" and thrown out. Gloria explained that that couldn't be farther from the truth. One of the main tenets of Al-Anon was to have love and respect for the alcoholic, and to keep the focus on one's own emotional and spiritual recovery rather than on changing or fixing the alcoholic.

A few hours passed, and Doug told Gloria he had to leave to drive back to Rhode Island where he would be getting up at 3:30 a.m. to catch a boat for another scuba diving adventure.

Doug's shyness kicked back in, but he really liked Gloria, so he got up the nerve to ask her for her phone number so he could call her and they could go to dinner sometime. Gloria gave Doug her number, Doug shook her hand and left.

Doug says that in his shyness, he fell back on his fourth-grade dance class etiquette, where they would shake their partner's hand after each dance.

Gloria was highly impressed with Doug's shaking her hand and being such a gentleman. She was also hopeful that he would call, especially since they shared some very important things in common; alcoholism, twelve-step programs, and a spiritual journey.

Several days later, Doug called and they set up a dinner date at a restaurant halfway between their two homes.

After that first date, they continued to date for four years. Nobody was in any rush to get married. They both felt it was rather sweet to enjoy the weekdays by themselves and spend weekends together. Doug called Gloria's place his "weekend country place," and Gloria would often bring her two cats down to Doug's place on weekends.

At just about the three-year mark, they talked about getting married but decided to move in together first. However, Gloria wasn't going to move in without an engagement ring. So that's what took place.

They've been together for twenty-two years now (married for eighteen), and they continue to share their love of adventure, spirituality, and sobriety.

The Guru's Spiritual Advice – "Join a Dating Service!"

Maria was in a place where she had met everyone's brother, cousin, and neighbor. She'd had a history of being with men who were either geographically, emotionally, or practically (married, engaged, or living with someone) unavailable.

It finally occurred to Maria that it wasn't them, but she who needed "fixing." So she went to therapy where she hit pillows with bats, and then entered a spiritual path that was challenging in every way possible.

Hearing Maria lament that she was still not in a relationship after years of working on herself, Maria's spiritual teacher said, "You need a marketing plan. Join a dating service." (This from a spiritual teacher!)

Maria's initial reaction was, "A dating service? Dating services are for losers! And they're certainly not the spiritual way to do things."

Her spiritual teacher went on to tell Maria that if she didn't join a dating service, she would have to admit to herself that she didn't really want to be in a relationship. He gave her ten days to join one.

Pissed off, Maria reluctantly joined a dating service. She met about fifteen guys. She had nothing in common with any of them, and was attracted to none of them.

She was about to give up when a profile came in the mail that piqued her interest. She showed it to a close friend of hers who said, "This is you, except this is a man."

They spoke on the phone and talked for an hour about Positano, Italy—and how much they both loved this enchanting town on the Amalfi Coast. He loved music and theater and loved to talk. He'd been in therapy and was self-reflective.

They met for a drink. He walked into the restaurant with a big hat and a long leather coat and beautiful eyes that looked right into Maria's. He was fun, he loved life, and was generous and not at all ordinary. And he was available in every way possible!

Maria and Andre have been together ever since and are having the time of their lives.

She Went to Texas and Came Home with a Russian

Michelle was twenty years old, in college, and pushing herself through her life in NYC. She was being stalked by a violent ex-boyfriend and was paranoid because earlier that year she had been held up at gunpoint in a store.

Michelle's sister determined that it was time to go out and have some fun, so they went to the Lone Star Cafe where they met two guys, Peter and Roy, with whom they laughed and danced the night away. Peter and Roy were originally from New York but had moved down to Houston, Texas. They told

Michelle that once she graduated she should "come on down" to Houston. They described it as a "boomtown" where it was easy to find a job without paying your dues.

Michelle liked how Peter and Roy were free spirits and she was desperate to get out of New York, so she learned to drive and packed up to go to Texas. She had no clue what she was doing, except that it felt right. She would later find out that she was being led by spirit. Michelle remembers her mother crying when she took off from her Park Avenue apartment. All her father had to say was, "Don't come home with a Texan."

About a year later, Michelle was settled into her own apartment. Due to her past experiences, she wasn't trusting of herself or of men. She felt disconnected and seemed to have physical relationships with men that didn't mean anything. She swore off men and even questioned her sexual orientation, but deep down she knew that her only desire was to be with a man who could see her for who she was rather than for her body. But she didn't believe she would ever find him.

Michelle became good friends with Peter and Roy, and one day Roy called and asked if she wanted to go on a double date. He told Michelle that he knew a guy he thought she would like. She told him that she doubted that, but would go with him to be supportive, because she knew he had the hots for a young lady in their housing complex. They decided that they would go to a jazz venue to hear Dave Brubeck. That way, if the dates didn't work out, at least they could hear some good music.

Boris sat across the table from Michelle next to her friend's date, a pretty, chatty blonde around whom the men seemed to flutter like butterflies. Michelle decided from the beginning that she didn't care, and just let herself get lost in the music. When Brubeck played "Take Five," Michelle noticed that Boris was looking at her. They were in the music together. After the song, Boris told her how he hated the dating game and just wanted to be himself. Looking directly at him for the first time, Michelle noticed his sparkly, almond-shaped eyes. His skin was smooth and tan, and she found she yearned to touch his hand. He was direct and genuinely funny.

As they talked, Boris told Michelle that a few years prior, he had emigrated from Siberia to Rome, and then found work in Houston. Roy and the chatty blonde took off, and Michelle and Boris found themselves talking on the steps of the theater until 4:00 a.m. They had lost all concept of time. Boris drove Michelle home in his blue BMW and asked if he could see her again. "That would be lovely."

They took it slow. Boris had an ex-girlfriend who didn't want to let him go and would often call in the middle of the night. Michelle's ex had no clue where she was, so she was free from her fears that he would be in her periphery. It helped to know that she and Boris shared recovery from difficult relationships.

Michelle began to trust and not wince when his soft hand reached to brush her cheek. If she wandered into a disconnected emotional state, Boris would gently encourage her to come back with his interest in learning more about her. He gave her pink roses which he insisted had to rest by floating in the bathtub at night. He was attentive and caring, and Michelle found that more and more she was able to relax and accept that.

Michelle's grandmother came to visit and took Michelle and Boris out to dinner. When Boris left the table to go to the men's room, Michelle's grandmother commented, "He's a bit gray, but I think you are going to marry him." Boris was thirteen years older than Michelle, but it didn't seem to matter.

Boris and Michelle married four years later, and that was thirty-one years ago. The joke in her family has been, "She went to Texas and came home with a Russian."

The "Chorus Boy" and the "Leading Lady"

Peter and Nancy met at the Light Opera of Manhattan, where Nancy was playing the soprano lead and Peter was in the chorus. At the time, Peter was in his early twenties and wasn't looking for the right person to spend the rest of his life with. In fact, he was enjoying being a single guy in the big city, and during the course of the production dated four different women from the cast.

One of those women was Nancy. On their one dinner date, it seemed that between Peter's not being serious about finding a long-term relationship and the fact that Nancy was also dating her leading man, it wasn't going to go anywhere. And it fact, it didn't. Not then, anyway.

Soon after, Peter left the chorus and got a job in advertising.

Even though he now had a "serious" job in advertising, Peter loved to sing, so from time to time he would appear in light opera productions. Four years after his dinner with Nancy, Peter was playing Grosvenor in Patience at the Village Light Opera and Nancy came to see the show because her good friend Lynne was playing Lady Angela. So, after not seeing each other for four years, Peter and Nancy met again after the performance.

Lynne didn't approve of the guy Nancy was dating at the time, so she suggested Peter call Nancy and ask her out. He called, they went out on a date, and have been together ever since.

Nancy also left "show business" to pursue a career as a fitness instructor and yoga teacher, and the two of them have now been together for thirty-six years in a marriage in which they definitely have equal billing.

"Would It Be So Bad for You to Pursue This?"

Emily, one of New York City's most prominent and successful jingle singers, had never married. She'd had one close call years before and had kissed a lot of frogs as well as dated some nice guys, but at age fifty-four she was still single and, frankly, quite content to be so. Emily's life was filled with music, friends, family, travel, and interesting, ever-changing work. She didn't have the sense that anything was missing in her life and was not looking to meet anyone.

Emily's best friend lived in Los Angeles, so Emily would take every opportunity to visit him there. Some other friends of Emily's had a house there, and knowing that Emily enjoyed visiting, would offer her their house free of charge whenever they traveled in exchange for Emily watching their cat.

On one such visit, Emily was sitting around the house one morning, scrolling through Facebook (which she had just recently joined), when she came across Robbie's picture.

Emily hadn't seen Robbie in a number of years, but she had known him through the music business. He was a well-known composer, arranger, and pianist, and their paths had crossed professionally on numerous occasions during the past thirty years. He had, from time to time, hired her as a singer, they had been in the same bands, and they had many of the same friends, so on seeing his picture, Emily thought, "I wonder what happened to him."

She knew that he was married to "rock 'n' roll royalty" (he was married to the daughter of a superstar singer/songwriter) and she had heard that he had closed up shop and left New York, but she had no idea where he had gone.

She clicked on his picture, and it said, "You must be friends with Robbie in order to see his profile." So she sent him a friend request.

Robbie responded right away through a private message that said, "Hi Sweetie!" Emily's first reaction was, "Hi Sweetie? Really? Interesting."

Now Emily had always liked Robbie as a person, but she'd always been a little intimidated by him. She was in awe of his talent, he had worked with just about every famous superstar on the planet, and he was part of a legendary music family. But the "Hi Sweetie" encouraged her to click on his profile.

Robbie's profile said, "Living in Sherman Oaks . . . single." And Emily thought, "Hmm. I wonder what happened?"

So Emily emailed him and said, "Hey, it's Emily. Was I supposed to know you moved to Los Angeles? I'm in Los Angeles. What are you doing?" She didn't even mention the "single" because, frankly, she wasn't thinking along those lines. She was just interested in catching up with someone she'd known from the past.

Moments later, the phone rang. Emily said "Hello," and the voice on the other end said, "It's Robbie." To which Emily said, "Robbie who?" Robbie said, "You just emailed me!" And Emily said, "Oh, sorry. I didn't recognize your voice. I wasn't expecting you to call."

They stayed on the phone for over an hour, catching up on what they'd been doing for the past few years. Robbie told Emily that he and his wife had decided to move from New York to Los Angeles so his wife could be back where she had grown up, and so that he could pursue more film work. Emily and Robbie talked like they were old close friends, and Emily couldn't remember ever having such a long conversation with him in all the years she'd known him.

At one point, Robbie said, "This is ridiculous. Why don't I take you out for a drink? In fact, why don't I take you out to dinner? How come we never did this? How come we've never just like gone out for a drink or something?" To which Emily blurted, "Well, you were never single before . . . oops . . . honestly,

Robbie, I don't know why I just said that, but there you have it."

So they met at a restaurant in Sherman Oaks, and Robbie told her the details of how his marriage, by mutual agreement, had ended. Emily found herself feeling like she was on a date, but as the evening progressed it became clear that Robbie was thinking of this evening as nothing more than having drinks and dinner with an old colleague. Throughout the evening he was giving her dating advice, asking, "Why aren't you on J-Date? Why aren't you dating? You were always the 'cute girl' and I always assumed you were involved with some great guy." So Emily thought, "OK, this isn't a date. But we're having a very comfortable, enjoyable time."

After dinner, they went back to Robbie's house, which was right across the street from the restaurant, and continued to have a lovely conversation. By one in the morning, with no sign of a move from Robbie, Emily said goodnight, told him it was great to see him and perhaps they would do it again sometime. She told him she'd be going back to New York in a couple of days and wished him all the best.

The next day, the people who owned the house Emily was staying in returned, and Emily moved out and went to stay with her best friend for a few days. She told him, "I went out with this guy. He's really cute. I always liked him. He's an old friend. It was very easy. But I don't know. Doesn't seem to be anything there." To which her friend said, "Listen. Would it be so bad for you to pursue this? He's single. He's handsome. He's funny. He makes a living. He's Jewish. And you could walk down the street holding his hand. He wouldn't be like some guy you're having a clandestine thing with. This is right. This is for you. You had a nice night. Don't you think you should pursue it?" To which Emily said, "Ah, I don't know." To which her friend said, "Well I think you're an idiot!" Emily thought for a minute and said, "I think you're right."

There was a dinner party that was happening before Emily was leaving Los Angeles, so she sent Robbie an email inviting him to go with her, suggesting that he might like to meet some people and that it might be fun.

Robbie never responded.

Emily assumed that this was proof that Robbie was not that into her, so she went to the dinner party alone and headed back to New York the next day.

It wasn't until weeks later that she realized she had sent the email to the wrong address.

Her best friend was getting married six weeks later to his long-term boyfriend, so Emily was planning a return trip to Los Angeles to be at the wedding. At her best friend's urging, she decided to try to contact Robbie once more, this time at the right email address.

She wrote to Robbie, telling him she was coming out for her best friend's wedding and had very little time, but asked if he would like to get together. His response was, "I really would."

Hm. This was encouraging.

The second time they got together, it was absolutely a date. And to make a long story short, they were together ever since.

In the three days Emily was in Los Angeles for her friend's wedding, she saw Robbie twice and had a great time. However, she still had her doubts. Robbie was living in Los Angeles pursuing film composing, and Emily was caring for her sick mother in New York. So although they had had a wonderful time together, Emily still wasn't 100% sure of where this was going. This much she knew. "He's a good person. He's an honest person. He's an upstanding guy. He's the kind of person I would want to be with. And he's cute and he's into me." In addition, she found out later that the reason he hadn't pursued her after their first dinner was that he was ending a dating relationship with someone else and he didn't feel it would be right to mix the two. So he had waited until that was officially ended to start dating Emily. Another sign that he was a solid guy.

Emily returned to New York, knowing she'd had a wonderful time with a great guy but not yet convinced that "this is my boyfriend."

And yet, as Robbie began calling her every night, she began to think, "Hm. Maybe I do have a boyfriend here."

A few weeks later, Robbie called to say that his whole family was coming East to have Thanksgiving on Long Island, and that he was hoping he and Emily might find time to get together. He then called back to say, "I just got a call to play at The Kennedy Center in Washington for a tribute to Barbra Streisand a week after Thanksgiving. I gotta figure this out. I guess I'll come to New York for Thanksgiving, fly back to Los Angeles, and then fly to Washington." To which Emily found herself responding, "That doesn't make any sense. Come to New York. Stay with me for a week and then go down to DC." The minute the words were out of her mouth, Emily thought, "Oh my God! What did I just do?" When Robbie said, "Are you sure?" Emily heard herself say, "Yes. I'm sure."

Emily became more and more sure, because in the interim between October and Thanksgiving, Robbie really courted her, calling every night, writing wonderful emails, and in essence, carrying on an old fashioned, love-letter courtship.

So, the day after Thanksgiving, Robbie showed up at Emily's studio apartment with a big suitcase. She met him at the elevator and he looked like a prince to her. They were practically making out in the hallway, and finally Emily suggested, "I think we should go into my apartment." Robbie agreed.

What followed was a remarkable week. Emily had had her piano tuned so Robbie could practice, and since the apartment was a small studio, Emily would leave the apartment when

Robbie needed to work alone. They spent the days and nights walking the streets of New York being a couple. Every day was easy and magical.

At the end of the week, Robbie went to DC, did the concert, and called Emily on his way back to California. On the phone, Emily said, "So, now what? That was kind of fun, right?" To which Robbie said, "I've actually never experienced anything like it. Our week was so amazing to me." Emily started to say, "So, I guess I'll see you . . ." and Robbie interrupted her. "Emily." "Yes?" "I'm completely in love with you."

Emily stopped breathing because: (a) she didn't know what to say; (b) she hadn't expected this; and (c) he'd really taken her by surprise, and until she responded she wasn't really sure how she felt. The next thing she stammered was, "Oh, oh. That's good. That's good. Because . . . I'm in love with you too."

So that was done, and Robbie ended the conversation saying, "OK. I'll figure this out." Robbie returned to Los Angeles, and from then on, one or the other was traveling across the country so they could spend a week out of every month together. Emily would have moved to Los Angeles in a second, but her mother was deteriorating and she couldn't leave her. Robbie made it clear that, of course, he did not expect her to. But Emily now knew this was the guy. When she told her best friend, he smugly said, "I told you!"

So they did this long-distance thing, and after three years of that, they both said, "What are we doing? This is crazy-making. One of us has to make a move."

Although by this time Emily's mother was deep into Alzheimer's, her physical health seemed to be holding steady and it didn't seem like she was going anywhere any time soon. So Emily definitely had to stay on the East Coast.

Realizing that this could possibly go on for a long time, Robbie finally said, "You know what? None of the jobs that I've gotten recently have been LA-centric, I've been doing tours with artists, and I could live anywhere." Furthermore, Robbie and his ex-wife had raised their kids in Bedford, a town in Westchester about fifty miles outside of New York City, and he'd always loved it there.

So Robbie suggested that he move East and they find a place together in Westchester.

It was settled. Emily flew to Los Angeles to help Robbie pack up and to be with him at his going-away party. No sooner had they started packing when Emily got a call saying her mother had taken a turn for the worse. Emily's mother's rabbi called soon after the first call and said, "I'm not a doctor, but if I were you, I'd get on the next plane." Emily did get on the next plane, but her mother passed while Emily was en route to New York. Robbie flew in two days later for the funeral, and he was Emily's rock. They had already found a house in Westchester, and as Emily thinks back on it, she has the feeling that her mother had said to herself, "OK. My work's done. My daughter has found the love of her life and she'll be living with him in Westchester. I can check out now."

Emily moved into the house on what would have been her mother's eighty-fifth birthday, and two days later Robbie, who had driven his car cross-country, arrived. It was rather a culture shock for Emily, who had lived by herself in her tiny rent-stabilized studio apartment in Greenwich Village for the past thirty-five years. But she jumped in with both feet, chose to put a period on the previous chapter of her life by giving up her New York apartment, and started her new life with Robbie.

As a footnote, after a number of years together, Emily naturally had the desire to marry Robbie. However, there was reticence on his side. He had been married before. This was working so well as it was. Why rock the boat? Emily had concerns about the fact that they were getting older and being a wife in medical, social, real estate, tax, and other situations was different from being a "girlfriend." But she was content to be with Robbie, so she didn't push it.

Due to his being very preoccupied with his work, Emily describes Robbie as a great procrastinator when it comes to getting little things done. To this end, she keeps what she calls a "Honey-Do" list of things she wants to make sure he gets done, including, of course, things she wants to make sure he gets done for her.

It was Emily's sixty-second birthday, and she woke up not in a good mood. She had broken her ankle a few months before and it was still hurting, she had cracked a tooth and was waiting for an implant, she was dealing with a bit of osteoporosis, and in general she was feeling lousy. When Robbie asked her, "What's the matter?" she said, "I'm old!" Robbie said, "You're not old. You're as old as me. We're sixty-two." To which Emily said, "That means we're 124!"

On her Honey-Do list, she wanted Robbie to take her to Home Depot to buy new towel racks and a sink. Robbie said, "OK! We're going to Home Depot!" He then proceeded to putter around the house, to shave, to do all sorts of little chores—in short, he was procrastinating. Emily was getting annoyed and finally asked, "What's taking you so long?!" Robbie said, "Well I did buy you a present." And Emily thought, "If it's jewelry, you're a dead man." Robbie was always getting her necklaces and bracelets, but there was only one piece of jewelry Emily wanted from him, and that was a diamond ring on the fourth finger of her left hand. Robbie repeated, "I have a present for you. Do you want it now?" Emily, still in her lousy mood, said, "Ugh. Fine. Give me the present."

Emily went downstairs to the living room and saw a big Tiffany box sitting on the table. And she thought, "Great, he got me a silver cuff bracelet or something." She opened the box but it was empty except for some bubble wrap. And Robbie said, "Ha, ha, fooled ya!" And then he reached behind his waistband and pulled out a ring box. Emily looked at it and thought, "Oh my God, oh my God." Inside the ring box was a velvet box, and inside the velvet box was a diamond ring.

Emily burst into tears. Then she said, "Wait a minute! Wait a minute! Does this mean we're getting married?" Robbie said, "Well, yeah!" To which Emily said, "Well are you going to ask me?" To which Robbie said, "Do you want me to get down on one knee?" Emily thought about it for a second and said, "You'll never get up. Just ask me!" So Robbie said, "Emily. Will you marry me?" And Emily said, "Yeah. OK."

They never got to Home Depot.

"You're Marrying the Wrong Guy!"

George, a freelance photographer working for a studio, was assigned to photograph a wedding. He had never met the bride or the groom.

When he walked into the dressing room at Temple Emanu-El and first laid eyes on the bride (Nan), it was as though he had been struck by Cupid's arrow. Smitten, the first thought that came into George's head was, "Why is she marrying somebody else and not me?"

George admits that during the wedding he was flirting, and at the reception he had the nerve to say, "Are you sure you really wanted to marry this guy? I think he's the wrong guy for you." To which Nan responded, "Well, I had to get out of my mother's house, he came along, and I married him."

As it happened, six weeks later, George was hired to photograph Nan's sister's wedding. Deviously determined to get closer to Nan, George suggested that Nan and her husband double date with George and a girl he was seeing at the time.

They went on the double date, and George and Nan and her husband became so friendly that her husband hired George to photograph their first anniversary celebration.

George nurtured their friendship, all the while just trying to stay close to Nan. It happened that they worked near each other in the City, so they met for lunch on several occasions. After a while, George told Nan that he couldn't be friendly with her and her husband anymore because he was really interested in her and it wasn't going to work out. George added that if Nan ever got separated she should call him.

Four years later the phone rang in George's studio. A voice said, "Hi," George said, "Nan?"—even four years later, he recognized her voice immediately—Nan said, "Yes," George said, "Are you separated?" Nan said, "Yes," and George said, "Let's have lunch." At the end of lunch, George said, "Let's have dinner." At the end of dinner, George went home with Nan and they were together.

But not so fast! George knew that with Nan just coming out of a separation and going through a divorce there was bound to be some rebound. And sure enough, after nine months, Nan gave George his walking papers. When that happened, George said, "I understand. Take as much time as you need, and when you're ready to come back, I'll be here."

At the time they'd been living in Greenwich Village, and there were a couple of restaurants that they frequented regularly. Six months later, George was in one of those restaurants with another date when Nan walked in, came up to the table, and said to George's date, "Would you excuse us? I'd like to talk to George for a few minutes." George's date had known that Nan and George had been an item, so she got up from the table. Nan sat down and said, "Let's go home." George said, "I'm on a date," to which Nan replied, "I don't care. Leave her here. Let's go."

George and Nan spent the next seven years living together, leading an idyllic existence in Greenwich Village. Nan often traveled to India for business, and George accompanied her at least once a year. George was working as a commercial photographer; they would both finish work, go out to dinner, drink, dance, have parties with friends, and travel to Europe, Asia and all kinds of places.

One day George came home and said, "This is all a lot of fun but it's getting boring. We need more. We have to have kids." To which Nan said, "Well, if you want to have children we have to get married." George said, "Fine."

So they got married, she got pregnant, and she said, "We need to live in the country."

So they moved to the suburbs.

George was in shock for a few years because the nightlife was so different (i.e., non-existent) from what he'd known in New York. But they made it, and thirty-eight years later they're still together and have a wonderful son.

It's NEVER Too Late for Love

After a long and happy fifty-seven-year marriage to her childhood sweetheart, whom she'd met at the age of fifteen and married at the age of twenty-three, Anne found herself a widow at eighty.

Just before her husband had died, they'd had a heart-to-heart conversation in which he'd told her, "Anne, you're a good person and a nice-looking lady, and you'll have other chances for a good life." Anne immediately responded, "No, John, that's totally unthinkable, I would never," to which John said, "Don't say that. If someone should come along who is worthy of you, I want you to go for it without guilt, and I promise I won't haunt you."

(In retrospect, Anne said that she feels it's tremendously important for all couples to have this final conversation while they're still alive, so they can be set free and go forward without guilt.)

A couple of months after her husband died, Anne went to a bereavement group. In this group, people sat in a circle and told their stories. The group was run by a woman, but on this day, because there were so many people in attendance, the group had been split into two sections, and Anne's section was run by a man named Bob, who was seated just to her left.

When it came to be Anne's turn to speak, she noticed that Bob seemed very interested in her story, listening in an extremely kind and attentive manner. He also seemed to be taking a lot of notes. Since Anne was sitting in a chair that was higher than Bob's, she was able to look over his shoulder and see that in addition to taking notes, he was doodling stars all over the page.

After the meeting, Bob stayed behind to speak with Anne. He asked her where she was living now that she was a widow. Anne said she was living in her home by herself. Bob told Anne that he was eighty-five years old and had been a widower for five years. He empathized with how difficult it was to live alone, especially after a long and happy marriage, adding that he thought it was not good for a woman who was widowed to be living in a house all by herself. He suggested that she might be safer and happier in a condo where there were more people around. At the end of the conversation, Bob pulled out his business card, handed it to Anne, and told her, "If you ever have a problem, call me." Anne took the card, thinking, "I'll never see or hear from him again." Meeting someone was the furthest thing from her mind.

Anne had been warned, at bereavement sessions she'd attended, that as a widow, she needed to be careful of men who might take advantage of her. But there was something about Bob that made Anne trust him, so when he asked her for her phone number, she gave it to him.

A couple of weeks later, Bob called. Anne found him very easy to talk to, interesting, and amusing. They both enjoyed that long phone conversation, and several other phone conversations that followed. After about the fifth phone call, Bob asked if he might take Anne to lunch later that week. Anne said, "Yes."

The day before they were to go to lunch, Bob called and said, "I can't make it at lunchtime tomorrow." Anne was disappointed. Her first date, and she was being stood up! But Bob quickly added, "Because I'd rather see you at dinner." Anne was a little suspicious, thinking, "Hmm, he wants to see me at night. Why is that? Seems awfully forward to me." But she quickly thought to herself, "Oh, I can handle it." So she said yes.

Bob took her to a very elegant restaurant. As soon as they sat down at the table, the waiter brought them a basket filled with bread, pastries, and tiny muffins. Bob said, "Ooh, these muffins are my favorites!" and proceeded to take a baggie out of his pocket, filled it with muffins, put it back in his pocket, took another baggie out, filled that one with muffins, and gave it to Anne to put in her purse.

Being on a first date where, as Anne put it, you're doing a lot of sizing up of the other person, Anne thought, "This is strange. Is he extremely frugal?" Since Bob lived in a very upscale community, Anne said to herself, "Maybe this is how millionaires get rich."

In retrospect, this was the only time Anne saw Bob be anything but ethical, generous, and magnanimous.

Bob started taking Anne out for meals regularly, about once every two weeks. At a certain point, Anne thought, "This is unfair that he's doing all the entertaining." So she invited him over to dinner at her house. She prepared a delicious meal of linguini, Garlicky Shrimp, salad, and strawberry cheesecake, lit candles, put on Mantovani dinner music, and waited for Bob to arrive.

Watching him come up the walk, Anne noticed that Bob stopped and looked into her car. She assumed he was checking to see if it was clean. When he came in, she said, "Good to see you. How are you?" and he said, "I'm very tired, Anne." At 85, Bob was still working as a contractor and real estate inspector, and he'd had a long day. So Anne said, "Well, dinner's almost ready, but while I'm in the kitchen, why don't you lie down here on the couch and rest." She got him a pillow and a throw and he lay back in the candlelit room with music playing. Later he said he was impressed by the care Anne had taken in the preparation of the dinner, in the atmosphere of her clean, neat home, and in the concern with which she treated him. Bob also told her that his previous girlfriend had never, never made dinner for him.

They began seeing each other regularly, and their relationship unfolded in a natural, comfortable way—without pain, without doubt. Whether at dinner, on the phone, or driving around town sightseeing, they enjoyed each other's company tremendously.

A few months into their relationship, Anne was diagnosed with a chronic but not deadly form of leukemia. She felt she needed to tell Bob, and was afraid that on hearing the news, he would run for the hills. On the contrary, Bob became more attentive, more interested in her, and closer to her. (Anne's doctors assured her that she could live a normal lifespan, in spite of her diagnosis.)

Bob began talking marriage. He was very up-front. He said, "I want to be with someone. Whether it's you or someone else, that's what I want. But I'm hoping it will be you."

One evening, as they were saying goodnight at Anne's doorstep, Bob was talking more and more about getting married. Anne said, "But Bob, I'm eighty and you're eighty-five. We're going to have health issues. Do you think it's wise to make such a commitment?" Bob immediately said, "Anne, it's so simple. If you get sick, I'll take care of you. And if I get sick, I know you'll take care of me. But for now, we're both well."

Shortly thereafter, Bob did have a health episode, and Anne said she wanted him to have a good checkup before they got married. Bob went to the doctor and got a clean bill of health.

Now there was nothing in the way of their getting married.

They had been dating for a year, and on Valentine's Day, Bob took Anne to a jewelry store to pick out a ring. When they went to apply for a marriage license, they found out that they were the oldest couple in the past five years to do so in Connecticut. Several newspapers interviewed them, and in one they said, "We've had 110 years of marriage experience between us. I think we should know by now what we're doing."

Anne and Bob spent the next ten years dancing, traveling, reveling in each other's company, and enjoying life. Everywhere they went, people could see the magic between them and would ask, "Are you newlyweds?" Some people even thought they might be having an affair and cheating on their spouses because they were so obviously in love.

At the age of ninety-three, Bob became ill, and as promised, Anne cared for him 24/7 for the next two years. Bob died peacefully in his sleep, lying next to Anne, at the age of ninety-five. Anne stayed in their house for a year and then moved to a beautiful assisted living facility nearby.

Who knows what romance or adventure might be next for Anne. After all, she's in good health, she's bright and attractive, and she's only ninety-two years old.

The Sailor of Her Dreams

Love had been a rocky road for Raissa. Career-wise, she was a successful New York actress, having played Christine in The Phantom of the Opera on Broadway as well as many roles both in New York and on the road. But Raissa's love life was another story.

After a marriage that ended in divorce and a rebound relationship that fizzled after a year and a half, Raissa was now in a relationship with a gorgeous body-builder/singer/actor/trumpet-player. The relationship had started out wonderfully, with him pursuing her, wooing her, and being very solicitous and respectful towards her. Raissa's self-esteem sometimes suffered from being with a man who was "more beautiful than she" (and who constantly needed to be told how beautiful he was), but she enjoyed his attentions, and with the two of them going to the gym constantly, she was in the best shape of her life. But now, as the relationship passed the two-year mark, his interest seemed to be waning, his attentions were intermittent at best, and Raissa couldn't tell if they were just in a slump or if the relationship was coming to an end.

Around this time, an offer came up for Raissa to be a headliner on a cruise ship in Hawaii for a year, and she jumped at it. When Raissa's boyfriend found out that she had been offered the job on the ship, he asked if she could get him a job too. In hindsight, Raissa now says they should have broken up at the two-year mark. But perhaps because of a combination of Raissa's wanting to be a good girlfriend and her self-esteem not being what it should have been, she convinced the producers to give him an audition, he got the job, and off they went to Hawaii.

On the ship, Raissa began to realize that her boyfriend was flirting with other women who were passengers, going out with them while they were onboard, and even sending postcards to them afterwards. Apparently, he would send the same postcard to each of them, because Raissa found a stack of unaddressed postcards, all with the same message on them. (The following year, when Raissa got back to New

York, friends told her that he had been doing the same thing when they were dating there.)

When Raissa confronted him and asked him, "If you knew that you did not want to continue this relationship, why didn't you just let me go away to Hawaii on my own?" he answered, "Well, I really wanted to go, I knew that you would always work, and I wouldn't work as much because I'm not as talented as you, so I wanted to take this opportunity." Raissa said, "So basically you were being selfish." To which he replied, "Yeah." At least he was honest. Raissa's "honest" reply was, "You son of a bitch!"

So they broke up, with the understanding that they wouldn't date anyone else on the ship's staff, as that would be too uncomfortable. They could, of course, date passengers, which gave her now-ex a great advantage because there were tons of cute girls constantly coming on the ship, and very few cute men.

So Raissa was basically at sea with a boyfriend with whom she had broken up, looking at a year with no romantic prospects that she could see.

Garrett was Second Engineer on the ship, in charge of fixing broken things and converting salt water into drinking water. Raissa had officially met him when she'd boarded the ship, and she would run into him frequently because she and the other performers sang at every Sail Away party and all the officers were always there.

A couple of weeks after Raissa and her boyfriend broke up, she and Corie, another girl singer on the ship and a close friend of Raissa's, were performing, and Garrett was standing by the bar in his dress whites grinning at them, raising his eyebrows, and raising his glass. When they finished singing, he came up to them and said, "You girls look like you're having fun up there!" to which both women simultaneously said, "Not really. It's acting!" Garrett, clearly flirting with Raissa, said "You know I sing a little." "Oh really?" "Yes, sometimes when I'm in New York I go down to the Duplex and sing." (The Duplex is a well-known piano bar in Greenwich Village with a large gay clientele.) So naturally, Raissa's next question was, "Are you gay?" "No!" was Garrett's immediate response. Garrett continued hitting on Raissa big time, but she was not interested at all.

Garrett began spending a lot of time hanging out with Raissa and Corie. Corie had also just broken up with her boyfriend back home, and she and Raissa were both reading the book Men Are from Mars, Women Are from Venus. When Garrett saw what they were reading, he said, "You know, there's a better book than that about relationships. It's called Men and Women in Conversation: You Just Don't Understand by Deborah Tannen."

Both women were exceedingly impressed that Garrett had read a book like that. When Raissa asked him why he'd chosen that book, he said, "Because I want to learn how to communicate better."

After this, Raissa decided she would start flirting back with Garrett, partly because she was enjoying the repartee, but probably more to make her ex-boyfriend jealous. Since Raissa was the Dance Captain of the show (in charge of rehearsing and keeping the show in shape), she said to Garrett, "You know what? I would do anything to have you videotape the show so I can see it." He said, "Really?" She said, "Yes," and he said, "Great."

Garrett videotaped the show for Raissa and afterward he said, "OK, I'm ready to claim my reward." Raissa said, "OK, what do you want?" and Garrett said, "I want a neck rub." Raissa said, "You know what? I'll do you one better. I actually know how to do massage, so I'll give you a full body massage. No funny business, but come down to my cabin and I'll give you a massage, with oil and everything."

Part of the reason Raissa was wary was that Garrett was a very good-looking guy, very flirty, and since Raissa had just broken up with a guy like that, she figured that was the last thing she needed.

But when she started giving him the massage, the facade broke down—Garrett dropped the playboy baloney and started chatting authentically, telling Raissa about his life and how he felt about a lot of things.

It was late, and they fell asleep side by side. Nothing happened; they just fell asleep. Garrett got up and left at 3 a.m. because he was scheduled to be on watch. Later, when Raissa was describing the evening to her friend Corie, she said, "He didn't even try to kiss me." Corie said, "Maybe because it means too much to him."

That morning at 8 a.m., Garrett called Raissa in her room and said, "What are you doing?" Sleepily, Raissa replied, "I'm sleeping." Garrett said, "No, what you really mean to say is, 'I'm going to get up and go have coffee with you.'" To which Raissa said, "No, I'm sleeping!" Garrett persisted, and finally Raissa said, "OK. I'll go with you. But I'm not putting on any makeup. I'm just going to get up, throw some clothes on, and go." Garrett said, "OK, I'll pick you up in ten minutes."

When Garrett arrived and Raissa opened the door, he said, "Wow, this is how good you look without makeup first thing in the morning!" Raissa thought, "Yeah, yeah. He's workin' it."

Garrett asked Raissa what she had planned for the day, and she told him she was going to go on shore in Kauai and play tennis later in the afternoon with her ex and Keith, the Cruise Director. Raissa asked Garrett if he wanted to join them and asked him if he played tennis. Garrett answered that he hadn't really played for a very long time and said, "Let's just go have coffee."

After they had coffee, Garrett took Raissa to a movie. They sat down and Garrett went to get popcorn and a Diet Coke. He came back and said, "Here, do you want some?" Raissa started to tear up. Garrett said, "What's the matter?" and Raissa said, "Nothing." When they left the movie, Raissa said, "I need to go pick up some water at GNC to bring to the tennis game." When they left GNC with the bags of water, Garrett said, "Here, let me take those," and Raissa started to cry again. Again, Garrett asked, "What's the matter?" and Raissa said, "Nothing."

She then said, "Why don't you come and play tennis with us?" Garrett wasn't even dressed for tennis, just wearing regular pants and boat shoes, but he asked who was playing. When Raissa told him her ex-boyfriend was playing (who Garrett of course knew since they were on the same ship together), Garrett said, "Well, maybe I'll go and play for a little while."

They started warming up and Raissa's ex and Keith said, "Why don't you play with Garrett?" Raissa said, "Well, I'm the weakest player, so shouldn't I be playing with the strongest player?" But they said, "No, you should play with Garrett."

They were playing doubles and at one point Raissa's ex was opposite her at the net and smashed the ball right into Raissa's hip. Raissa was fairly new at tennis and didn't realize that it was very poor etiquette for a man to ever smash the ball at a woman.

At that point, Garrett picked up his game and he and Raissa beat the pants off of their opponents. The other two guys were very thrown because they were good tennis players and were upset that they'd been beaten by someone who not only hadn't played in such a long time, but wasn't even wearing sneakers. Garrett left because he had to be on watch, and the other two said, "He's played before," to which Raissa said, "No, he told me he hasn't played much."

When Raissa got back to the ship she said to Garrett, "Boy, you really freaked those guys out. You told me you hadn't played before," to which Garrett said, "I didn't say I hadn't played before, I just said I hadn't played in a while." Raissa said, "Well, they said you must have been a really good player," to which Garrett said, "Well, I was the state doubles champion in high school," quickly adding, "but it was New Hampshire, so it was a very small state."

Later on, Garrett said he really hadn't been interested in playing tennis, but he was not going to let Raissa be around her ex-boyfriend without him. He added that he had not been planning on showing off, but that once Raissa's ex hit her with the ball all bets were off.

Months later, Garrett asked Raissa why she had cried when he offered her a soda in the movies and when he offered to carry her water. Raissa told him that when Garrett had done those things, she realized how far down she had let her self-esteem go with her ex-boyfriend. In the last months she had been with him, there had been several occasions where she had been struggling with heavy bags and he had not offered to help her, but would run up to some cute passenger and grab her bags. Or when Raissa would ask for a taste of what he was eating, he would sigh and say, "Why don't you get your own." Garrett's naturally considerate behavior caught her off-guard and made her see that she had taken for granted that this kind of behavior couldn't happen. With

That night Garrett said, "Can we hang out tonight after you're done singing?" He came to her cabin in his boiler suit (a big, clumsy pair of blue overalls) and said, "I brought some of my favorite music to show you. I brought some pictures to show you. And . . . can we cuddle?" Surprised, Raissa said, "Sure."

Then Garrett said, "I want you to share one of your favorite CDs with me." Raissa put on Laurie Beechman singing "Listen to My Heart."

(Author's Note: I'm especially fond of this part of the story because, as it happens, I wrote the song "Listen to My Heart" and I produced Laurie Beechman's CD.)

Garrett said, "Wow I love the song and I love her voice." Months earlier, Raissa and Garrett had discussed the fact that Raissa had played Christine in Phantom of the Opera, and Garrett had said that he wasn't that familiar with the show, because he hadn't liked the lead soprano's voice, but he really liked Raissa's. (Raissa, by the way, sings in many different styles. Not only does she sing soprano, she can belt it out with the best of them.)

Garrett really loved the CD, and later, when Raissa left the ship for a while and he was still on the ship, she made him a mix tape of it.

That night they talked for hours, he showed her pictures, and that was the first night he kissed her. From that time on, they were inseparable.

Now Raissa and her ex had had an agreement that they wouldn't date anyone on the ship. But Garrett told Raissa that her ex had sat down with Garrett late one night at the midnight buffet and said, "It's OK with me if you date Raissa." Garrett's response was, "Thanks, man. Let me know if you want a tour of the engine room." So their relationship was "condoned."

They had been dating for about two weeks when Raissa looked over at Garrett and thought, "This is not going to work." Raissa had plans to go to L.A. to try her hand at the TV and film side of the business, and Garrett was from the other end of the country. At that precise moment, out of the blue, Garrett asked, "How do you feel about having kids?" A bit taken aback by the question but struck by Garrett's directness, Raissa answered: "Well, I always thought I would have them, but at this point I'm somewhat ambivalent about it. In truth, I'm probably leaning more towards no." Garrett replied, "Yeah, I really like kids but I'm not so interested in having them either." It was very clear to Raissa that it had been important to Garrett to have that conversation.

Shortly after that, the cruise line decided to put the ship into dry dock for refurbishing, so they sent Raissa to New York to await being reassigned to a sister ship.

Garrett, being Second Engineer, brought the ship into dry dock and came back to the City in time for Raissa's birthday.

Since Raissa had given up her New York apartment, and since her ex had immediately been assigned to another ship, Raissa crashed in her ex's apartment. Garrett stayed with her in that apartment, and that week brought Raissa up to New Hampshire to meet his parents. Raissa remembers being really impressed by this, because her ex had taken forever to introduce her to his parents.

Soon it was time for Raissa to leave for Hawaii to finish out her shipboard contract. Garrett walked her to the gate, and with tears in his eyes, told her he loved her. Raissa had already told Garrett she loved him, but had never heard those words from his lips.

Raissa and Garrett talked to each other almost every night from Hawaii to New York on the ship's 800 number. Garrett had decided to go to medical school, and had been accepted at the University of Rochester. This would create even more complications of future distance for the two of them.

After about a month of being on the ship again, Raissa realized that she really didn't like this ship as much as she had liked the previous one. (The previous ship had had a special magic. Among other things, it was the ship on which the movie An Affair to Remember had been filmed.)

In one of their ship-to-shore conversations, Garrett asked Raissa, "Are you having fun anymore?" When Raissa answered, "No, I'm really not," Garrett said, "Well, that's because I'm not there." Raissa shot back, "Well that's pretty egotistical of you . . . but it's true." Garrett then said, "Well, why don't you come home?" Raissa gave her notice and called Garrett to tell him that she'd given her notice and had made arrangements for the cruise line to fly her to LaGuardia Airport in New York. Garrett said, "Why don't you have them fly you to Rochester? You're going to arrive in LaGuardia and think, 'What am I doing seven hours away from Garrett?'" Again, so egotistical! But Raissa said, "You know, you're probably right." So Raissa told Garrett she'd get a flight to Rochester, visit for a few days, and then take the train down to New York City.

Raissa had not been in Rochester a day when she noticed that a close friend of hers was music directing a show at a theater in Rochester. She called him and he said, "I've been trying to reach you. Where are you?" When Raissa said, "I'm in Rochester," he said, "I've been trying to reach you because I wanted you to play a part in the show."

Raissa thought, "Well that would be convenient." Raissa took the part in the show and lived with Garrett from then on. They stayed in Rochester through Garrett's medical school, with Raissa commuting to New York on occasion for auditions and work. After medical school, Garrett did his residency in New York City and his fellowship in Birmingham, Alabama.

Garrett and Raissa have now been married for nineteen years. Garrett is a prominent New York City sinus and facial plastic surgeon, and Raissa has continued her theatrical and recording career and become a fixture in the New York cabaret community. And none of it would have happened if they both hadn't gone to sea.

Garrett Weighs In

Here's the story from Garrett's perspective.

Trying to figure out what he wanted to do with his life, Garrett had spent the past six years doing various jobs: working on ships, designing nuclear submarines, and, for two years, working in real estate. He finally decided he wanted to go to medical school. He applied, was accepted to several, and chose Rochester.

With seven months until school started, Garrett signed up as an officer for one last six-month stint on a ship that was making weekly tours of the Hawaiian Islands.

He figured he'd make a little extra money, take a month off, and then head up to Rochester to begin medical school.

On the ship, Garrett worked two four-hour shifts a day, 8–12 in the morning and 8–12 at night. Since the ship hit the same five ports every seven days (Garrett made this tour twenty-six times during his six months on the ship), there was plenty of time to go ashore, roller blade, see a movie, go to the beach, climb a volcano, and basically have a great time.

As an officer, Garrett was permitted to mingle with the passengers and go to all the shows on the ship. (Regular crew had to stay in their own area during their time off.) So Garrett would put on his dress whites and hang out at the bar during the shows. The bartender liked Garrett so he never got a bill.

Garrett was into a sambuca phase, so he would go to the shows, order a special sambuca drink, and sit and watch the performers. He was extremely taken with Raissa and with her voice and her performing, so he made it a point to strike up a conversation with her.

As his show-going and the conversations that followed became a habit, Garrett began ordering two sambucas, so he could have one waiting for Raissa when she got off the stage.

Raissa was still dating the boyfriend she had brought on the ship with her, but the relationship was fraying. Garrett was friendly with Raissa's boyfriend, and they would sometimes run into each other at the midnight buffet (which they called "midnight cheese," because by the time Garrett and the entertainers got there, all that was left was cheese). The boyfriend was already thinking about dating other women, so he told Garrett that it was fine with him if he dated Raissa. Garrett was more than fine with the idea.

Garrett started hanging out with Raissa and her girlfriend Corie, going to the beach with them at every chance. According to Garrett, Raissa was not interested in him romantically. She knew he had a crush on her, but she didn't think he was particularly good-looking and he was a ship's engineer and she didn't see a future in dating a sailor. But Garrett kept going to the beach with her, and paid careful attention to her conversations with her friend Corie.

One day, Raissa and Corie started talking about their "lists"—what they wanted in their next relationship. A lot of Corie's list had to do with practical things, like having a valid driver's license and credit card, stuff that seemed to be below the food chain of what Garrett thought of as important. But Raissa's list started with, "Believes in God" and went on to include, "Needs to read books, be attentive and emotionally available, do more than work out and talk about weights, etc." Garrett took careful notes. He had his doubts and questions about

God, but he began to realize that he had every other quality on Raissa's list. So he told her, "I have everything on your list except the first thing, and I'm working on that." He then began to purposely talk about self-help books and classics he was reading, he'd bring up subjects that he knew were on her list, and, in general, act in ways he knew she would appreciate, all to impress her with how right he might be for her. He was determined!

Raissa began to be impressed, and slowly Garrett won her over.

Of their first kiss, Garrett says it was like the line from The Princess Bride which (to paraphrase) said, "In all of history there were only three kisses that were the most passionate. This one blew them all away!"

Although Garrett was infatuated with Raissa, at first he was not thinking it was going to be anything long-term or serious. But when Raissa left the ship before he did and headed back to New York, he realized that he truly missed her. So he wrote her a letter saying, "You're going to get back to New York and you're going to wish you were with me." By that time Raissa liked Garrett as much as he liked her, so when he arrived in Rochester, she flew up to visit him and was immediately cast in a show that was playing there.

Right after the show finished, Phantom of the Opera called and asked if Raissa would fill in as Christine on the tour. Raissa flew to New York that day to rehearse, and then the tour left for its first stop . . . Rochester!

Raissa continued with the tour, and six months later, a year after they had first met on the ship, Garrett flew out to Cincinnati and asked Raissa to marry him.

Her Resistance Was No Match for His Persistence

Suzanne was done with dating. After several disastrous relationships, she was living contentedly by herself in Brentwood, California. She was happy with where she was living, was happy with what she was doing, and she had an adorable little malti-poo dog named Milito, short for mi abuelito which means "my little grandpa."

George, on the other hand, having been divorced for a number of years, was definitely looking. In fact, he was studying and taking his cues from a book on how to meet and date women.

George had seen Suzanne passing his house while she was walking her dog on several occasions. Suzanne had no idea that George existed.

One day, Suzanne was walking her dog, and passed this strange-looking older man who was futzing with his Lexus in his driveway. Strange-looking because his eyes looked a little crazed (probably because he was nervous), he had no hair, and was dressed in a Flashdance sweatshirt (he had just come from the gym). And older because he was, in fact, seventeen years older than Suzanne.

It never occurred to Suzanne to be interested in this man, nor did it occur to her that he might be interested in her. As Suzanne put it, "Every woman has a resume in her head of what her ideal partner would look like, and he didn't fill the bill at all."

But George came bounding down the driveway, said "Hi! What's your dog's name?" and proceeded to have an animated conversation exclusively with her dog. After a while he included Susanne in the conversation, and after a brief chat, Suzanne moved on.

As he watched Suzanne walk away, George thought of a Clint Eastwood film in which Clint's character had said to himself, "If the woman looks back, she's interested in me. If she doesn't, she isn't." Suzanne looked back. As it turned out, she wasn't looking back at George but at something else, but it was sign enough for George to decide to keep pursuing her.

George liked Suzanne. As soon as she left, George ran upstairs to write down Milito's name and the date and time they had met so he would have that information when they met again.

But according to his dating guide, the next thing he was supposed to do was not to appear to be too anxious. The way the book suggested he do this was to not do anything for at least ten days. So George, who knew what time Suzanne usually walked her dog, did not appear in his driveway for the next ten days.

On the eleventh day, George excitedly went down to the driveway early, to be sure not to miss Suzanne if she happened to take her walk before her usual time. He cleaned the dashboard of the car. He straightened up the back seat. He brushed off the car mats. He moved the CDs that were in the trunk into the car. He moved the CDs that were now inside the car back into the trunk. But no Suzanne.

Just as he was about to give up, she came around the corner. George said, "Hey Melita!" (mispronouncing the dog's name to sound like the coffee filter) "How ya doin'?" and once again proceeded to talk to the dog. (Suzanne remembers thinking, "Oh God. Not this guy again!") But they began talking and after a brief conversation, George said, "Would you like to go out to dinner sometime?"

Suzanne, having lived in L.A. a long time, and naturally cautious due to past experiences, immediately said, "Lunch!"

George handed Suzanne his card but Suzanne did not give him her number. Suzanne got home and immediately misplaced the card. She put it somewhere and forgot where she put it.

It didn't really matter, because she'd made up her mind that she wasn't going to call him.

In the meantime, each of them had traumatic events occur. George had a burst appendix and was in the hospital for ten days, while Suzanne had lost a very dear friend and had to attend and travel to four different memorials.

About a month and a half later, when Suzanne finally got back and resumed her dog-walking, she passed George's house and was surprised to see George's car looking dirty and uncared for. Knowing how obsessed George seemed to be about his car (after all, he was always out there doing something to it when Suzanne would pass), Suzanne's first thought was, "He's died. He loves his car. There's no way he would let his car get this dirty. He must have died." But she couldn't find George's card, and anyway, she'd resolved not to call, so she let it go.

Now, in L.A. it's very rare to run into someone you know in a store or on the street. There are too many cars, too many people; it hardly ever happens. But one day, Suzanne went to the ATM at her bank in Brentwood, and there he was!

He was wearing a big loose sweater and looked a little odd. He told Suzanne, "I've just had surgery and I'm feeling a little tender around the gills." But George casually asked (continuing to follow the don't-be-too-anxious rules of his dating guide) whether Suzanne would like to take him up on that lunch they'd talked about months before and meet him over the weekend. Suzanne said "OK," and they made a date.

As Suzanne was leaving to meet George for their lunch date, she thought to herself, "If this guy turns out to be a jerk, I'm leaving after coffee." She felt really great with her life, she didn't need anybody, she'd had a rough history with dating, and she wasn't going to disrupt her life getting involved with someone she wasn't really interested in.

But George surprised her. He was funny, he was very smart (Suzanne always found smart really sexy), and after lunch he asked her to walk with him to her favorite bookstore. At the bookstore, he asked Suzanne to help him pick out a great cookbook so he could learn to cook vegetarian. (He actually was buying the cookbook so he could cook a meal for Suzanne to impress her, which he later did.)

They had a really fun time, and from then on George began to up the ante, consistently saying, "Let's do this. Let's do that." Their next date was in Malibu, for a hike in the mountains. George brought a picnic with him. George brought a knife with him. Suzanne, ever-suspicious, thought, "Great, I'm out here in the middle of nowhere with this man I hardly know and he has a knife. What if he's a killer?" Looking at his physique she found herself thinking, "Can I take him if he attacks?" Fortunately (and really not surprisingly, Suzanne's wild imagination notwithstanding) George used the knife only to cut bread and cheese.

Soon after, George took Suzanne to his office (he was a high level financial executive for an institutional financial management company). The office was on a cliff overlooking the Pacific Ocean, the design was all Japanese, and if George had taken Suzanne there to impress her he had succeeded.

At one point, George took Suzanne out on the beautiful balcony overlooking the sea and kissed her. And Suzanne thought, "Wow! He's good at this! I think I might keep him."

They went out on several interesting dates, not simple dates, but things like concerts and special events. (Suzanne suspects they were all suggested by George's dating guide.)

After about five or six dates, George asked Suzanne if she wanted to go to Hawaii with him for Christmas. Her first response was, "Great, I'd love to do that." But then her old doubting self kicked in and she thought, "Wait a minute. You're not like that. You don't know this guy. You've barely met him and you're going off to Hawaii with this guy? What if he's taking you there to just leave you there? You'll be stuck on an island across the ocean with no money." But the excitement of going to Hawaii and the fun she was having with George won out, and off to Hawaii they went.

They had a wonderful time. George found a condo on the beach in Maui and they spent their days enjoying each other's company, not doing much—just being together. It was like being on a cloud. Suzanne was a little puzzled by it all, given that they were such different people, but for some reason it worked.

Right at the end of the trip, Suzanne had to be in Sacramento to be at the celebration of her parents' sixtieth wedding anniversary. Suzanne had a very large family (seven brothers and four sisters) and a very complicated and challenging family dynamic. The tight scheduling between the end of the trip to Hawaii and this event in Sacramento meant that Suzanne and George had to fly directly to Sacramento. This also meant that George was going to meet Suzanne's entire family!

Suzanne briefed George on how challenging certain relationships in her family could be, and asked him to protect her. And boy did he protect her! He was constantly by her side, to the point where he scared her family, but Suzanne was grateful. If a conversation was too difficult, he would think of an excuse to shepherd her away. Frankly, she had never felt so safe and comfortable being around her family.

Suzanne had one more test that she felt compelled to put George through. Art was very important to Suzanne, and she wanted to make sure that George understood and appreciated art the way she did. So she took him on a date to the Los Angeles County Museum of Art.

Suzanne showed George one of her favorite paintings. George's response was, "No, I don't particularly care for that." They wandered off in different directions, and after a while Suzanne found George sitting on a bench in front of a massive painting with a lot of browns, grays and tans and little dots, and George said, "Now this is a painting I like." "Ew," thought Suzanne. "I don't like this at all." But Suzanne said, "You like this painting? Tell me why." And George proceeded to go through a whole complex and erudite explanation of why he liked the painting." He clearly appreciated and was well-informed about art at a depth that most people aren't.

George had passed another test and Suzanne thought, "OK, this is working."

Shortly thereafter they were living together.

About a year later, George's company reorganized and George was out of a job. He found a job in New York, and asked Suzanne if she would be willing to move there with him. Suzanne, by this time, was in graduate school, studying landscape architecture and interning with a world-renowned landscape architect. Years before, Suzanne had had an experience where she had left Sacramento to move to Los Angeles with a man and it had turned out to be a disaster. (Still, it had brought her to Los Angeles, which ultimately turned out to be a great thing.) But she loved George, and after careful consideration she chose, to the great dismay of the man for whom she was interning, to pull up stakes and move East with George.

Suzanne and George took a trip to Vermont, and as they were walking through the woods, they came upon a prayer place where there was a circle, each quadrant of which represented a different religion. Suzanne remembers thinking, "This would be a good place to propose." And sure enough, George turned to her and said, "Suzanne, will you marry me?" Suzanne responded, "Of course I'll marry you. I was just thinking that this would be a good place for you to propose." George was crestfallen because he had thought he was being so creative asking her there. But he'd gotten the answer he'd hoped for, so all was well.

Shortly thereafter they found a house, got married, and have been together for eighteen years.

All It Took Was One Piano Lesson

Dave, a studio musician, arranger, pianist and songwriter, got a call one day from Stacy, a singer/songwriter. They had never met or spoken before.

The reason Stacy had called Dave was that a friend of hers (who just happened to be Dave's ex-girlfriend) had played

Stacy some song demos of hers (which had been done by Dave) and Stacy said, "Why don't my demos sound like that?" Another mutual friend suggested that Stacy call Dave to find out what sounds he used on his synthesizer.

Stacy and Dave had a number of long phone conversations about music, and at one point Stacy said, "I'd like to play piano better. Perhaps I should take some lessons from you."

Dave happened to be talking to his ex-girlfriend, with whom he had maintained a friendship even though they had broken up, and when he mentioned that Stacy was going to come over and take piano lessons, his ex, who knew Stacy, said, "Oh no. If you meet Stacy, you're going to fall in love with her and I'll never see you again."

Stacy came over and asked Dave to teach her how to play classical music. Dave immediately said, "I don't know why you'd want to learn that. It has nothing to do with songwriting and you're a songwriter."

Stacy played Dave one of her songs, and he said, "It's a good song, but it needs some reshaping." Unlike many writers who would be defensive about the constructive criticism, Stacy was open and receptive, and they began to work on the song together.

On that day, right then and there, they both instantly knew that they would be collaborating for a long time. They have been living together, writing songs and making music for decades.

Dave said he doesn't know what his life would have been like if he hadn't had that "chance" meeting with Stacy. They're perfect for each other in every way.

Overnight Success!

In June of 2013, Anika was at the lowest point of her life. She was about to turn forty, she had just gone through a breakup, and was despairing of ever finding love or having children, something she had always longed for. Her theater career felt like it had stalled, and in the previous year she had earned an amount close to the poverty level. It seemed like she just couldn't keep doing what she was doing, hoping for a call from her agent that would solve everything.

Anika decided to quit show business, get a "normal people job" that she could rely on (with health insurance she didn't have to worry about losing), and figure out a way to have a baby on her own. She had a good cry, weeping for her career and the life she had thought she would have. Then she let it go and went to bed.

The next day (literally the next day, not the next week, not the next month—but the very next day) her agent called to say that she had gotten cast as Cynthia Weil in the new Broadway show, Beautiful: The Carole King Musical. And a month after they opened, Anika's dresser, who helped her with her quick changes and had heard her lamentations about online dating and lingering exes, asked her if she wanted to be set up on a blind date. He was a trumpet player named Freddie, and he was a friend of her dresser's husband. Anika figured if both members of a couple thought this guy was a good idea, then that seemed optimistic. She said, "Absolutely."

A few weeks later, Anika went to BB King's in Times Square to watch Freddie play. He was fantastic. And hot. And she kept thinking, "Please, just let us have something to talk about!" She need not have worried. When Freddie found Anika afterwards, he immediately cracked a joke that made her laugh out loud, and they didn't stop talking 'til they closed down the joint. It was the best first date she'd ever had.

Four months later, Anika moved in with Freddie. Two months after that she was pregnant. And on the one-year anniversary of their first date, they got married.

So Anika guesses a call from her agent did, in fact, solve everything. But it wouldn't have, if she'd hadn't done her due diligence. She'd spent twenty years sowing seeds and creating fertile ground, and then in one crazy season, everything blossomed. Now, her cup runneth over! (Oh, and she did get a Tony Award nomination for her performance in Beautiful.)

How She Met Her Mother

Margot was born to unwed parents in Boston and was given up for adoption when she was two weeks old. Although she was certainly well-raised and cared for, rejection became a constant and central theme in her life.

When she was six, her adoptive father, who was an alcoholic, left their home and moved far away. Her mother remarried, and Margot immediately began calling her stepfather "Dad." However, after a period of time, he too left.

Throughout her childhood and into her college years, Margot maintained strong defenses against the rejections she'd experienced. When asked whether it bothered her that she'd been adopted, she'd say, "No. I'm special. I was chosen." When another friend who'd had alcoholic parents decided to go to a meeting where children of alcoholics helped one another, Margot agreed to support her friend by going along with her. In the meetings, Margot sat silent, not saying a word about herself. When others in the group asked her to share her story, Margot demurred, saying, "I'm just here to support my friend."

Her fear of rejection made Margot not even consider looking for her birth parents. But something happened that began to push her in that direction.

One evening, a close friend of Margot's gathered a group of girlfriends around her, including Margot, and told them that she was pregnant. She wasn't married. Now Margot and her close girlfriends were attending a Christian college, so even the idea of abortion was out of the question. Margot assumed that her friend would give the baby up for adoption, as Margot's parents had done. But to Margot's surprise, her friend decided that she would keep the baby and raise it herself. Even when her boyfriend left her, even when she lost her job, even when she had appendicitis during the pregnancy, Margot's friend maintained her resolve to keep and raise the child.

When the child was born, Margot looked into his face, and among the many questions she had about this "miracle," the one that rose to the top of her mind and heart was, "Where did you come from?" This immediately led to, "Where did I come from?" Margot began to think about all the things she wanted to know about her background. Why was she the way she was? Did her parents act, look, and talk like her? What had been going on in their lives that caused them to give her away?

Reluctantly, Margot began researching agencies that reunited adopted children with their birth parents. She filled out an application, but didn't send it in. (In the book Margot has written about this experience, The Girl in the Orange Dress, she jokes that usually an agency has a better chance of reuniting you with your birth parents if you send in the application.)

Finally she sent it in, defending herself against rejection by rationalizing that the chances were incredibly slim of her ever finding a match. The good thing about this agency was that they would only call you if a match was found, so there would be no chance of a direct rejection from them. Rather than giving her own address, she gave her adoptive mother's address and her adoptive father's address, again once-removing herself from getting "bad news" directly. Her rationale for this was that she was living with several girlfriends from college, including the girlfriend who'd had the baby, and since her situation was temporary she'd probably be moving on and her address would soon not be valid.

A week later the agency called her original stepfather and through him found Margot. The agency had found her birth mother. Her birth mother had also applied to the same agency and was anxious to talk with her. Shortly thereafter, Margot was on the phone with Pam, her birth mother. Pictures were shared, stories were told, they arranged to meet, and they have remained close ever since.

Ya Gotta Kiss a Lot of Frogs!

Eugene, a gifted pianist, arranger, and music director, was what you truly might call "unlucky in love." Hailing from Fort Worth, Texas, a town with a large Hispanic community, he'd always been attracted to Mexican girls. At the age of fifteen, he began to date a girl who had very strict Mexican parents. The parents did not speak English, and Eugene and his girlfriend were required to always take one of her younger brothers or sisters with them everywhere they went. At the age of twenty-one, they decided to marry.

From the beginning, the marriage was extremely challenging. Eugene's wife, and his wife's family, seemed to be just waiting for him to get a "real" job, and they certainly didn't think that being a musician qualified. As the years went by, and Eugene became more devoted to and successful at making music, the rift between them grew wider. Even having two children did not bring them closer together. After fourteen unhappy years of marriage, they finally called it quits and got a divorce.

Soon after, Eugene's career took him to New York City. Being a dyed-in-the-wool Texan, he wasn't particularly fond of living in New York, but that's where the jobs and connections commensurate with his talent were, so off he went.

Eugene's brother headed up a big church choir in Corpus Christi, Texas, and he would invite Eugene down periodically to perform with them. During one of these visits, Eugene met another Mexican girl. She was an alto in his brother's church choir, and Eugene liked her very much. Although they lived in separate cities and didn't see each other that often, they eventually became boyfriend and girlfriend, with Eugene returning periodically to Corpus Christi to be with her. Then, impulsively, they decided to get married.

Eugene's wife-to-be had always dreamed of a big wedding in the Corpus Christi Cathedral, which was her home church and which was where Eugene's brother was music director. But complications around the fact that Eugene's first wife had never filed for the annulment that Eugene had given her money to procure caused them to have to be married in the Methodist Church nearby. This was a big blow to his very-Catholic wife. There was tension in the relationship, which was exacerbated by the fact that Eugene's wife was afraid of New York, and thus never came to live with him there. On the few occasions when she did visit Eugene in New York, for important events in his career, she felt extremely uncomfortable, saying New York was way too big for her. She even thought Fort Worth was too big for her. She just couldn't fathom the show-business lifestyle Eugene lived; the celebrities, the hours, and the fast pace. It quickly became apparent that their marriage was not going to work, so two years after they were married, they decided to part as friends.

Eugene next thought he would try online dating services. He signed up for match.com, but had terrible experiences. For his first date, he thought he and the woman he'd met on line might meet at Starbucks, but she insisted he meet her at a particular restaurant. She told him to wear a jacket and tie. It turned out to be an extremely trendy, noisy, and expensive place, and he ended up dropping well over a hundred dollars on dinner. Other unpleasant experiences followed, so he decided to drop match.com and try eHarmony.com instead.

When Eugene got to the "relationship status" question on the eHarmony application, there was no box for "divorced." The closest thing was, "separated" so that's what he checked. He received a notice that they couldn't accept him because he was still married. He wrote back saying that he was, in fact, divorced, and would have checked that had there been a box for it. But they wrote back to say he had to be divorced for a certain amount of time in order to sign up. Eugene gave up.

Not long after his online debacle, Eugene began work on a production of The King and I. The show, of course, had many Asian cast members, and Eugene found himself drawn to a number of them. They were charming, polite, sweet, and funny. Knowing about Eugene's history with Mexican women, one of the cast members, a gay Filipino man, suggested to Eugene that if he liked Mexican women and Asian women, he might really like Filipino women since the Filipino culture was a combination of the two. He then told Eugene, "I'll bet you'd like my sister" and showed him a picture of a beautiful girl. Eugene said, "She's gorgeous!" to which his friend, the gay dancer, laughingly responded, "Fooled ya! That's a picture of me in drag!"

At any rate, his friend told him that there was an Asian dating service where Eugene might meet Filipino women. Eugene had never heard of such a thing, but figuring he had nothing to lose, he signed up.

Eugene soon saw a girl he wanted to meet, and began chatting with her via Skype. Unfortunately the girl's microphone was not working, so they could only type to each other.

At first their conversations were pleasant. It was a little challenging for Eugene because, since there was a twelve-hour time difference between New York and the Philippines, he had to do his Skyping between the hours of midnight and 5 a.m. After a few conversations, the girl began asking him for money. It started with $20 to get something to eat; $50 to buy something; $100 to help her uncle who was in trouble. Eugene began to get suspicious that he was being taken for a ride. Then he received several Facebook posts from other people on the dating site saying that the person he was talking with was actually a she-male. When he confronted her she denied it, but when he falsely threatened her, saying he had connections in the Philippines and she could go to jail for extortion, the "relationship" quickly ended.

The next girl he got "involved" with very quickly began asking him for money. First she wanted $1,500 for a green card. Then she told him that she had come to the US, she was standing in Columbus Circle, and he should meet her there right away.

It was a gorgeous, sunny day in New York. Calling her bluff, Eugene mentioned how soaked she must be getting standing there in the pouring rain. "I know," she said. "That's why I need you to come and get me." Eugene has no idea what plot she was cooking up or who would have actually been there to greet him had he shown up, but the relationship ended right there.

Not one to give up, Eugene tried once more. This time he connected with a woman named Liza. Her Skype worked perfectly well. She seemed to live in a nice house which he could see on the screen. She had two lovely children. The first time they spoke they talked for five hours. Day after day, they talked from midnight to 5 a.m. She never once asked for money. She told him that two women for whom she had worked in the Philippines were now living in Queens, and connected him with them by Facebook. Eugene asked Liza if she had a visa, and she told him she had a travel visa but not a green card. After a time, she made arrangements to come over to New York to meet Eugene.

The night before Liza was to leave for New York, her family threw her a big party. Eugene attended via Skype, meeting her brothers and other family members. When she arrived in New York, she and Eugene hit it off immediately. Eugene was looking kind of scruffy, and Liza said, "I have to clean you up." And boy, did she mean it! First she took him for a haircut and had him shave his beard. Next she completely cleaned up his studio apartment, and organized everything in it. Accustomed to eating every meal out, Eugene was now treated to her delicious home-cooked meals, which not only were better than the ones he ate in restaurants, but also saved them a lot of money.

Many of Eugene's show-business friends, knowing of his history, severely cautioned Eugene not to bring Liza over. But as each of them met Liza, they fell in love with her.

Liza and Eugene spent the next few months enjoying each other's company. Liza was clearly happy to participate in Eugene's life, and it soon became apparent that they were meant for each other.

Liza's travel visa was to expire on Valentine's Day, so they decided to get married several months before that date, to allay any suspicions that this might be a "green card" marriage. Their green card interview went extremely smoothly, as it was obvious that these two were the real thing.

This prince had to kiss a lot of frogs, but he never gave up, and found his princess in the end. They continue to live "Happily Ever After."

As a footnote, Liza later told Eugene that she had signed up for the dating service on the very day the two of them first spoke, and that he was the first person she spoke to. After her one conversation with him, she cancelled her subscription and spoke exclusively to him, via Skype. Clearly, this was meant to be.

The Black Belt and the Garbage Man

As the highest-ranking student in the karate class she'd been a member of for twenty-five years, Jen was the first black belt her instructor had ever produced. Because of her ranking, Jen was usually the first person new people met when they came through the door on their first day. So over the course of all those years being a dedicated member who hardly ever missed a class, Jen had met just about everyone on their first day.

As a rule, guys who came in the door for the first time portrayed themselves as macho, egotistical men, chest out, muscles flexed, all pumped up, grunting in their best gorilla-like-supposedly-intimidating-voice, "I'm here to see the instructor." It was always baffling for Jen to see these guys portraying themselves as these "I can kick your ass" kind of people.

Another thing that was somewhat upsetting to Jen was that when she'd greet people at the door, in her full karate regalia, including, of course, her black belt, they would look her up and down and almost without fail ask, (in their stupidly deep voice) "Are you a black belt?" And Jen would think to herself, "Seriously?" And she would ignore the question.

Scenes like this would happen, almost without fail, whenever a new guy walked through the door. These guys typically fit a certain pattern, ignoring martial arts etiquette in class, talking back to every senior belt, disrespecting the class, questioning the teaching, even asking Jen out or trying to flirt. It was as though they thought they were in a pick-up joint rather than a serious martial arts studio.

From the beginning, Jen was immune to all these macho-men's "charms."

So one day, Jen was off in the corner near the door working on some techniques alone, when the door opened and in walked a new guy. Thinking to herself, "OK, here we go again. Let's see how gorilla-ish this dude can be," Jen walked over to greet the guy at the door, and as she always did, said, with a smile, "Hello. How can I help you?" And he humbly said, with no fluff whatsoever, "Hi. I'm here to see the instructor." Jen thought to herself. "Wow! This guy is so handsome and has such a quiet, respectful nature. . . ." Needless to say, after twenty-five years of greeting people at the door, her heart skipped a beat.

This guy, whose name was Paul, ended up joining the class. Jen found out that one of guys in her class whom she'd known for eighteen years had invited him. She also found out that Paul had known this guy for the exact same number of years, but she and Paul just never knew each other.

Anyway, Paul's joining the class gave Jen a different feeling about being a member of the class. Each day, Jen would get dressed for class with an unusual type of excitement—sort of heart palpitations, hoping Paul would be there so she could be in the same space with him. Karate class is hands-on, and Jen would be really excited about being hands-on with Paul! Unlike so many other men, Paul was extremely receptive to the ways of the class, and seemed unfazed being "hands-on" with Jen

One day, an older Caucasian man (Jen is African American) came through the door. He had to be in his seventies. Jen greeted him with her usual smile and said, "How can I help you, sir."

The man told Jen he was there to pick up his son. Jen asked him who his son might be, and he said, "Paul." Then Paul's father asked Jen how Paul was doing in the class, and Jen said, "He's progressing very nicely and he's very good at following directions." In essence, Jen was really impressed that this beautiful new guy had asked his father to come to the class. Much later, Jen would reflect on how lovely it was that she'd been able to talk to her father-in-law before any of them knew they would be "family" one day!

Now at this time, Jen, who'd been married for years and had two children, was separated from her husband and was in the middle of getting a divorce. She hated the feeling of being single and hated the idea of dating even more. She'd already told the universe the type of guy she wanted, and her list of requirements was extensive. He'd have to be respectful of himself and of others, he'd have to be taller than Jen, he'd have to accept her children, and most of all, her children would have to accept him. He'd have to come into the relationship with at least an equal amount of assets as Jen, be a non-smoker, a non-drinker, and, getting incredibly specific (they do say you have to ask specifically for what you want), Jen hoped he'd be a builder or a garbage man! Jen wanted a builder because she'd know he could build a house and fix everything that might go wrong with it. She wanted a garbage man because, in the 1991 sitcom Roc, the leading character was a married garbage man whose house was furnished with items he found on his garbage route, and his wife was proud to show it all off. Since Jen is frugal, she knew she would love being married to a garbage man and getting free, gently used items.

At that time, Jen was working at a car dealership. One Saturday, in walks Paul with his teenaged nephew. Paul had no idea Jen worked there—so what a coincidence! Jen greeted them at the door, sat them at her desk, and they talked about what kind of car Paul was looking for. To build rapport (because there was no talking to each other in class—class was about karate and karate only), Jen asked Paul what line of work he was in. Paul told her he worked for his family who owed a garbage company! Holy Moly!

Wanting to find a way to get more of a connection going with Paul, Jen asked him if he had the capability of clearing junk out of storage bins at the condo complex where she was the president. He told her he could definitely do that. So, of course, this was Jen's opportunity to ask him for his number.

When Paul gave Jen his number, he wrote down his first and last name. To Jen's surprise, Paul's last name was the same as hers! They'd both been born with the same last name. Jen also asked Paul if the car was to be owned jointly with a wife, and he said he had divorce papers in the works—same as her! So many things they shared in common!

The next day, Sunday, Jen took the opportunity to call Paul to make an appointment for him to give her an estimate on cleaning out the storage facility. They arranged for him to come over the next day after work. When he came there on Monday and they were down in the basement together, Jen was having a lot of sensations being so close to him alone in the basement area.

When they came out of the basement and went over to his pickup truck, Paul got in and, as they were ending their conversation, said, "Oh, by the way, do you like chocolate?" and handed Jen a little box that had two chocolate hearts in it. Jen thought, "Hmm . . . I wonder if he likes me . . . ?"

Two days later, on Tuesday, Jen called to follow up with the basement cleanout issue and thanked Paul for coming by. They ended up staying on the phone for probably an hour. Jen learned that Paul was currently living alone with his dog, Buddy. Well, Jen was living with her children and her cat, Buddy!

On Wednesday, their mutual friend invited Paul and Jen to dinner after karate class. Jen sat catty-corner from Paul and really got to take a good look at him during the dinner. What she saw, as she watched him talking and laughing, was that this man was good-looking, had character, had shiny dark hair, was low key, was a gentleman, and was respectful of Jen and her young daughter, who was also with them at dinner.

On Thursday, Jen found another excuse to call Paul, and again, they talked for about an hour. Throughout their conversation, Jen was listening very closely to how Paul would answer her questions. Jen asked him if he goes out on weekends, gets drunk, and brings women home for casual sex (like guys at her job said they did every weekend). Paul said he definitely does not do that.

Paul then told Jen he used to drink a whole lot. At this point Jen said to herself, "This is definitely a deal breaker—it's done—he didn't pass my test!" Paul went on to say that he hadn't had a drink in seventeen years and that he will not touch the stuff—never again! OK. So maybe he would pass her test.

Jen really started zeroing in on certain things. She even asked him what size bed he sleeps in, and he said, "A queen." (Jen thought to herself, "That's a really big bed for one guy.") The final question that really got her thinking this might be the "one" was when Jen asked him to tell her what he missed most about being married. Paul said he missed coming home to the smell of a home-cooked meal after work. Wow! That's exactly what Jen missed about being married . . . Having her husband come home to the smell of a home-cooked meal!

After Jen got off the phone, she mentally took inventory of everything she had learned about Paul over that past week:

- He's in garbage—perfect!
- Divorce papers in the works—mine too . . .
- Dog named Buddy—My cat's name is Buddy!
- Misses home-cooked meals—I miss cooking them . . .
- Does not drink—neither do I!
- He said he's a procrastinator—My dad wrote the book on procrastination!
- Has same last name as me—What a story this can be . . .
- Sleeps alone in a big bed—I could fix that!

The only thing Jen was confused about was that she had not expected her perfect man to come in this particular package. She then realized that when she'd given the universe her very specific criteria for the perfect man, she'd neglected to mention he should be 6'2" and dark-skinned African American. She'd just thought that was understood. "Whoopsy!"

Anyway, Jen went to sleep that night thinking about everything. During the night, Jen was told by her subconscious mind that this is a good man and she should not let him get away. It became crystal clear that Paul was the guy she'd asked the universe for. Once she had that information, she could barely sleep. She feared that overnight another woman could come along and swoop him up! Morning just couldn't come fast enough. She got up on Friday morning, knowing she had to move quickly, and jumped right on it.

Jen actually took the risk of calling Paul on Friday morning to ask him out. He was quite surprised to hear from her in the morning. Trying to sound calm, Jen asked Paul what he was planning to do after work. Paul told her he was planning to go home, take care of his dog, take a shower, make himself some pasta, and get his clothes ready for work on Saturday. Jen said, "No, I mean, are you going out anywhere?" Paul said, "No," so Jen said, "Well let's go somewhere!" He seemed a little stunned that Jen had been forward enough to ask him out. But he said, "OK," and that was all that mattered.

They had a wonderful evening, they talked, they laughed, and Paul was a gentleman. They went to Blockbuster to pick out a video, and at some point while they were in there, Jen slipped her hand into Paul's and he took hold of it. Jen felt electricity go through her body. Then Jen asked Paul how he felt being with an African American woman, and Paul said, "It feels great!"

Traditionally, Jen had always felt nervous and out of whack on first dates and even during relationships, but being with Paul felt so natural. After they picked out the video, they went out to dinner and talked about what they wanted out of a relationship. What they found was that they both wanted a lot of the same things. Then they went back to Paul's place. It was all very surreal yet magical. They both knew they wanted to be together for the long-term, but neither of them spoke it.

Jen saw Paul again on Saturday and Sunday. Now she knew she'd have to tell her karate instructor about their relationship. She knew it would cause trouble because she's a senior member of the class and not there to pick up men. She knew he'd be very upset because he knew she was just getting out of a marriage. Jen went to her instructor on Monday and asked for a sit-down meeting with him. When she told him she and Paul were seeing each other outside of class, her instructor was not happy about the news—for all the right reasons. But as time went by, Paul and Jen proved themselves, and he quickly got over it.

After a few months, Jen brought Paul home to meet her children. She'd informed him from the beginning that if her kids didn't accept him or like the idea of her being with him, for any reason, she would have to end their relationship. Paul said he understood.

When Paul walked into Jen's house, her son, who was seventeen at the time, got up and hugged him with a smile. Not the reaction she was expecting. Her daughter was cordial, and stayed close to Jen. She was not as welcoming because her father had always been her best friend. However, she did not reject Paul. She was just standoffish. She had the perfect reaction for a little girl going through her parents' divorce.

Shortly after meeting Jen's children, Paul told Jen he was in love with her. Jen told Paul it was too soon, but he said it wasn't too soon for him. Well, too soon or not, Jen was clear she loved Paul too. They started talking about getting married. They wanted to get married immediately, but there were things they had to work out. Also, they didn't want to cause a ruckus with their families, being newly divorced and jumping right back into marriage. So they told each other they would wait a year and then get married. And that's what they did.

Jen's daughter has grown to adore Paul, and their household has always been peaceful. Paul didn't try to come in and take over, make the kids call him Dad, and all that nonsense. He always leaves for work in a good mood and always comes home the same way—talkative and friendly. The four of them have had great times together. They all eat at the table as a family for dinner, they go to movies together, take road trips—they do everything together. Twelve years later, they're still going strong.

The Walls He Had to Break Through Were His Own

Growing up as an overweight, nonathletic, artistic, gay kid with a family that loved him but disapproved of his being gay, Richard entered early adulthood with some serious self-esteem problems. The way this lack of self-esteem often played out was that Richard would put up a wall when meeting people, to ensure that he wouldn't get hurt if they rejected him. This made it extremely difficult for him to find a relationship.

It was the day after Labor Day, in Portland, Oregon, and Richard, as he often did, was going out for a beer with his best friend Dave at a local bar. On this particular quiet Tuesday evening, Lee, a friend of Richard's, who Richard knew as an avocational singer, was also at the bar. When Lee wasn't singing, he was working at his real job, as a dietician in a mental institution. That evening, Lee was with his friend Bud, who worked with him at the mental institution. (Friends of Richard's like to say that Bud's working at a mental institution was what made him a perfect match for Richard.) At any rate, Richard and his friend Dave joined Lee and Lee's friend Bud for a beer.

The moment Richard met Bud, bells went off. But typical of Richard and his self-doubt, there were two kinds of bells: bells of excitement because Richard was very attracted to Bud, but also bells of warning because Richard was so afraid of someone he liked not liking him back that he would immediately find everything possible wrong with them so that if they weren't interested he could tell himself that it wouldn't have worked out anyway. In this case, Richard thought, "What kind of person would go out drinking on a weeknight?" (Perhaps Richard didn't notice that he himself was out drinking on a weeknight.) Next, Richard noticed that Bud was very quiet at first. That could be a problem, or not, depending on how much Bud liked other people to talk, because Richard certainly did talk a lot!

Usually this kind of internal criticism would stop Richard in his tracks. But perhaps because he had tried to come to terms with his defensive behavior during that summer, and had been able to correctly recognize his thoughts for what they were—bricks in a wall to keep him from being open to relationship—Richard hung in there. Instead of walling himself off, he asked Bud about himself. This was a major step for Richard. Richard found out that Bud was a runner. (So was Richard. Running was one of the ways in which Richard had lost the excess weight he'd carried throughout his childhood.) Richard found out that Bud played volleyball with a gay league. (Richard definitely did not do anything like that!) They even found that they had another mutual friend, a pianist, in common. Bud told Richard that the reason he was out for a beer with his friend Lee that evening was because they had gone for a run together. Richard's first inclination was to judge that, thinking, "Well that's stupid. Why would you go running and then ruin it with a beer?" But in his newfound nonjudgmental, open state of mind, he thought, "Well maybe it's a good way to replenish carbs after exercise."

Having broken his own personal barriers by showing an interest in Bud, Richard still didn't know if Bud was interested in him. But one thing Richard did know was that he was certainly interested in Bud. Deciding not to act desperate (another self-defeating behavior Richard often exhibited), he waited a week and then casually called his friend Lee and asked about joining him and Bud for a run. It took Lee a week to arrange it, and then they ran along the waterfront, Richard and Bud talking all the way. (Bud definitely wasn't as quiet as he'd first seemed.) Richard realized that he was right. Bud really was someone special. But Richard still didn't know if Bud felt the same way about him.

After a few more runs over the next few weeks, Richard got up the nerve to ask Bud if he would like to see a movie sometime. Bud said yes. They first met for tacos in a funky Mexican restaurant so crowded that they had to sit at the bar, and then walked to the movie. Richard wondered if this guy was always as nice as he seemed to be, so he decided to find out by asking him out again before the end of the evening.

Rather than taking the chance of asking Bud how he felt, Richard made the decision to hold back the reins and just let things unfold naturally.

Being a professional singer, Richard tends to think of the early phases of a relationship in terms of song lyrics: "Getting to Know You," "I've Got a Crush on You," "I Can't Get You Out of My Mind." Richard had gone through all three of these phases with Bud, but he still wasn't sure how Bud felt. So Richard decided to up the ante by inviting Bud over to his house for a belated birthday celebration, as Bud had just celebrated his birthday a few days earlier. Richard bought a special birthday cake from his favorite bakery, picked up a few books he knew Bud would like to read, and made homemade spaghetti. Bud liked the cake and the books. Well, thought Richard, two out of three ain't bad.

But more importantly, that evening Richard found out that Bud liked Richard. That was the start of a relationship that has lasted for decades.

Bud Weighs In

Growing up in a traditional white, middle class family, Bud did as he was expected. He finished high school, got a job, and married his childhood sweetheart. His marriage lasted only four years, and when it ended, Bud knew that it was time to move on with life and explore who he really was, including his sexuality. To give himself a fresh start, he moved to Portland, Oregon, where he went to work in a psychiatric hospital.

In Portland, Bud met his first gay man who was very interested in introducing this suspect "straight" guy to the gay life style. For the next few years Bud explored the gay scene, even playing on a gay men's volleyball team which ultimately ended up going to the Gay Olympics in San Francisco.

During his years working in the psychiatric hospital, Bud became friendly with a man named Lee, who worked in food service. As he got to know Lee better, Bud learned that Lee was singer and was also a runner. Before long, Lee and Bud started running together in downtown Portland.

On one particular day, Bud and Lee went for a run after work. It was an extremely hot day and after their run they decided to go to a nearby bar and cool down with an ice-cold beer. This was not something they usually did. In fact, this was the first time Bud and Lee had gone for a beer after running.

As Bud and Lee sat talking and enjoying their beer, two guys entered the bar. Lee commented that he knew one of the guys. The guys turned out to be Richard and his friend Dave. As the four of them chatted, Bud learned that Richard was also a runner. As Bud remembers it, he and Lee invited Richard to join them the next time they ran. (This does not jibe with Richard's recollection that he had to call and ask if he could run with them.) At any rate, about a week later, Bud, Richard, and Lee ran together for the first time. Bud remembers them chatting pleasantly as they ran, but doesn't remember thinking anything more of it than just guys getting together for a run.

The three of them began to run together regularly. On a couple of occasions, Lee was unable to join them, so Bud and Richard ran alone. It was during those times that Bud got to know Richard as a person. As they continued to run together, they became friendlier.

Bud will never forget the time when a mutual friend of Bud's and Richard's invited them over and they hung out in the hot tub. Their friend was a pianist, and he and Richard had similar connections in the music world to talk about. At one point the friend asked Richard to sing something. Bud claimed he almost had a heart attack when Richard opened his mouth to sing. He couldn't believe that anyone could sing like Richard did.

Richard and Bud continued to hang out together, and Bud remembers that one night, after a volleyball game, Richard met Bud and his team at a bar for a beer. Somebody asked Bud if he and Richard were an "item" and Bud told him no. The guy went on to ask if Richard was fair game, and Bud said yes.

Then, in October, a few days after Bud's birthday, Richard invited him over to his house for dinner. During the course of the evening, for the first time in his life, Bud felt like he'd met someone who really liked him for who he was. Bud began to recognize that Richard was a loving, caring and generous soul, and that is the Richard that Bud fell in love with. The rest is history.

Literally a Dream Come True

Alan actually saw Janis in a dream before he met her. About a year before they met, Alan had a dream about this absolutely adorable girl who was beaming with joy. She was shopping! (As anyone who knows Janis would attest, that dream was spot on.) He woke up, certain that someday he would meet this wonderful girl.

And meet her he did. Alan is a composer (there's no question you've heard of him), and in the fall of 1971 his rock ballet, Children of the World, was produced by the Downtown Ballet Company. Alan was at the piano, about to rehearse one of the sections of the piece, and in walked Janis Roswick, a new dancer who had just joined the company. One look and Alan knew she was the girl of his dreams.

Ironically, Janis was having a similar sixth sense about Alan as she entered the rehearsal space. Although she had spent her life dancing to scores by classic composers, this was her first time working with an original score, not to mention having the actual composer involved. During early rehearsals she had said to herself, "I can't believe someone wrote this music. It's incredible." And when she heard Alan was going to be at rehearsal, she said to herself, "Now, don't go falling in love with him just because he's the composer." Unfortunately (for Alan at least), she didn't have quite the same love-at-first-sight experience that he had when he first saw her. Alan was a pretty weird sight in those days: with long hair, wild eyes, and hippie attire, his "look" was disheveled and he had a totally wired energy.

Janis, on the other hand, was a vision of perfection. She was pretty much Alan's opposite. She spoke in such a proper way, and was neat, clean, disciplined, and centered. And supposedly she had a boyfriend. Ouch!

Shortly after that day, the company was performing at Trinity Church down in the Wall Street area. Alan went to watch this performance, mostly as an opportunity to see Janis again. As the dancers came off-stage, Alan approached Janis and said, "Hi." She said, "What are you doing here?" He said, "Waiting for you." She said, "I have to meditate."

And she sat in a pew, eyes closed, hands neatly folded in her lap, doing her twenty-minute Transcendental Meditation practice. Alan sat patiently until she breathed in and out a few times a bit more deeply and opened her eyes. Janis turned toward Alan and he blurted out "So . . . Howya doin'?" A small pause and she replied, "I'm fine . . ." Alan said, "Wanna see a movie or get a bite or something?" And Janis said, "OK."

They went to see a pretty dark art film, Il Decameron, directed by Piero Paolo Pasolini, accompanied by another couple who were dancers in the company. After the movie, Alan and Janis made a date for a few days later. On that date, during their dinner at an Egyptian restaurant called Cleopatra's, Janis told Alan she would break up with her "boyfriend." (Yay!)

He was so gone over this girl. And, by some miracle, she kind of liked him too!! Two weeks later, they moved in together.

Janis continued to dance as a principal dancer in her dance company, and Alan Menken went on to write so many of the Disney movies and Broadway shows we all know and love. They've been together for forty-four years, married for forty.

You Can't Fight the Truth (or a Tight Pair of Tennis Shorts)

On a day early in August of 1988, Kevin, an actor, kissed his wife goodbye and headed off to St. Louis, Missouri, to appear in a production of Candide. Kevin and his wife had met in college, had been married for five years (together for nine), and were living a happy life together—working actors with plans for fame, family, and fortune in whatever order the universe might choose to provide them. In fact, Kevin's wife was planning to join him in St. Louis in a week to work in the costume shop of the theater where he was performing. Life was good.

Kevin had been asked to perform in this production by his good friend, Terry Reiser, who was choreographing the show. Arriving at the small one-bedroom apartment in the two-story complex where the entire cast would be housed, Kevin, now left to his own devices, was ready to explore the local campus and take on his first tennis victim. Putting on his white tennis shorts, with racquet and tennis balls in hand, he set out to find his friend Terry for a couple of games before dinner.

Kevin had never thought of himself as handsome or as the head-turning type. But he did, at the age of twenty-six, have a few natural assets worth noting, or at least that might catch the eye of someone looking: a full head of natural blond hair, muscular well-shaped soccer-playing legs, and an ass you could bounce a quarter on (which incidentally, hasn't totally given over to gravity at age fifty-five).

Kevin owed his friend Terry big time! Candide was the third job she had hired him for in the course of two years. As he crossed the grounds of the apartment complex, Kevin saw Terry lying on the floor of her apartment (or what Kevin thought was her apartment), waving to him through the sliding glass door. Kevin bounded over the lawn to greet her and walked into the apartment through the open glass door.

Stretched out on the floor beside Terry was a young man whom one might characterize as attractive, handsome even, and definitely in good shape—in fact, in very good shape . . . that is, if one were paying attention or at all interested in that sort of thing. Terry got up to hug and kiss Kevin hello. The attractive-handsome-even-and-definitely-in-good-shape-if-one-were-paying-attention-or-at-all-interested-in-that-sort-of-thing guy never moved from his stretched-out floor position, but smiled and nodded a friendly, "Hello." Terry made the customary introductions: "Kevin, meet James. James, meet Kevin." Hands were shaken and contact was made. As Kevin remembers it, glances were shared, smiles were "real," some inappropriate thoughts were silently entertained, nothing else was said other than "Hello," and in a few moments Kevin was out the door, on his way to play tennis.

In retrospect, Kevin couldn't have more perfectly planned the impact his white, high-cut tennis shorts, blond hair, "real" smile, and back-side-best quality would have. But none of this would ultimately matter to the friendship that was about to happen that had now begun in that instant.

As James remembers it, he was almost thirty-three years old, dripping with sweat because it was nearly 100 degrees in St. Louis and the dumpy apartment he was staying in had no air conditioning except for a crappy window unit. The unbearable heat was the reason he was lying there immovable, prone on the living room floor alongside his friend Terry. But the temperature was not the only thing that was hot in that apartment. James was a hot guy, attractive and muscular—the former because of good family genes for which he was eternally grateful, and the latter because he had an obsession with going to the gym and working on his body. James was also a happy guy, thanks to continual work in the theater that included a starring role on Broadway as Riff in the revival of West Side Story, as well as many varied roles in other productions in New York and around the country.

James says that as he was lying on the floor of his apartment, he saw a cute guy coming across the yard . . . actually, more masculine than the word "cute" reflects. As Terry waved the guy over, she said to James, "You are going to just love this guy!" More prophetic words were never spoken.

James recalls hardly being able to see past the short, exceedingly short (they don't make them this short anymore) men's tennis shorts Kevin was wearing. The assets they were covering were a temporary distraction. In contrast to what Kevin recalls, James actually remembers their having a conversation. After their introduction to each other, Kevin asked Terry to play a few sets of tennis with him. Terry said that because she had a production meeting to attend, she would have to take a rain check. Kevin looked at James and asked if he played tennis. James swears that he said, with a sincere and sweet smile and just a tad of innuendo to ensure that his words had a double meaning, "No, but I'd like to learn." James thought it was a pretty good opening line and well played by any measure, but his overhead lob indeed went right over Kevin's head. Before James knew it, the tennis shorts, or rather Kevin, went out the door. At that point, James looked at Terry and said, "Is that my gift for coming to St. Louis?" Terry, with a stern face, responded, "He's straight! He's married! And his wife will be here next week!"

All was lost.

Rehearsals for Candide began, with James playing Candide and Kevin playing the Rich Jew. This was especially significant since it meant that James would be killing Kevin at every performance, and Kevin would be throwing James into a burlap bag, kidnapping and abusing him. As Kevin likes to put it, the "getting to know you" phase of their relationship involved kidnapping, murder, and straight out brutality, all in the name of fun, of course. At any rate, rehearsals were filled with a teenage sort of roughhousing between James and Kevin, and provided a safe way for them to bond, in full view of the rest of the cast, their enjoyment of each other's company bearing no risk or the trappings of being anything else other than a kindling friendship.

Outside of rehearsal, activities included daily gym workouts (together) which James insisted Kevin take up, while James actually did acquiesce to taking a crack at tennis. Rehearsal breaks and dinners were spent with other cast members as well, but Kevin and James were rarely not together. The first week flew by, not filled with anything of particular note, just two young guys hanging out, unthreatened and unconcerned that their instant and immediate friendship was anything more than that. The arrival of Kevin's wife at the end of the first week only added to the ease of their being together in groups or in their more private post-rehearsal schedule. If it sounds titillating, it was, but that can only be applied in retrospect. It was certainly not sexual in the least. It was far more important than sexual—it was chemical and meaningful.

The four weeks of rehearsal flew by, as rehearsals typically do, and their clique of friends grew to about six, including the one mutual friend who had brought all of them together, Terry. As the opening approached, they were all looking forward to that day in just one week that would truly be a free day to just hang out and explore St. Louis.

Candide opened and was an instant hit with critics and audiences alike. What was further clear to everyone who witnessed the production was that the hunky, sexy, curly-haired male lead was a real head-turner. James' romping around on stage nearly naked with his equally wonderful and attractive female costar left everyone feeling a bit warm.

Right after the opening, Kevin's wife flew back to New York, returning to her own acting career, while the cast settled in for the month of performances ahead.

One of the things James and Kevin did together in their spare time, either with other cast members or by themselves, was bowl. Unexpectedly, it was bowling that caused both their greatest joy in being together and their first direct confrontation. Fighting over the "correct way" to keep score, they not only nearly came to blows, but they recognized a fiery passion and sense of competition in each other. Back in James' apartment after their first big "bowling fight," they continued to argue over who had "really" won the day, finally bursting into laughter and admitting their mutual stubbornness. After that, they more and more often enjoyed bowling with just the two of them, undistracted by others. Strike, strikeout, gutter ball, spare—argue—reset, new frame . . . new game. In fact, a truly new game was happening, and they were completely unaware!

When not bowling or performing the show, Kevin and James were at the gym. Their workouts had only intensified as Kevin got stronger. He could now lift as much weight as James, so they had another daily competition in addition to bowling. Who could lift more? Who could do more reps? Who had the lower body fat? Who weighed more . . . or less? There is no more perfect time to weigh oneself than right after an intense workout at the gym, sweating out every last ounce of water before jumping on the scale. The amazing result of this particular competition was that Kevin and James were exactly the same weight, both weighing in at 162 pounds. Now with all of this togetherness, working out, sweating, being together in the locker room, it might seem like this would have been the perfect place or time for something "else" to happen. But it didn't. Not until an accident changed things.

With one week left in the run of Candide, James injured himself onstage while doing one of the required acrobatic somersaults and flips. Though he managed to finish the performance, he was seriously hurt. Very early the next morning, Kevin drove him to a doctor for X-rays, chiropractic care, and more. James had completely thrown out his back. That was bad enough, but there was also a domino effect to this injury. It had never occurred to the producers to have understudies assigned for the production, much less an understudy rehearsal. After visiting the emergency room, James and Kevin returned to the theater and provided the producer with a full report of James' condition. Based on what the doctors had said, it was evident that James was in no shape to go on that evening, even with all of the drugs he was now taking to deaden the pain. In the true spirit of the "show must go on," Kevin drew the short-straw to play the part of Candide that evening. James went to bed. Kevin went to rehearsal. As Kevin raced through learning the part, he was surprised that by osmosis alone he knew most of the music by heart. That may have been due to his watching every scene or singing along backstage with every song. But what Kevin hadn't learned was the dialogue, choreography, and about half of the staging. Rehearsal finished and Kevin rushed backed to the apartment to check on James' condition. Heavily drugged and barely moving,

James answered the door. The next instant would be that life-changing conversation that would set the course for the next twenty-eight years.

Kevin proposed a deal with James. If James could somehow manage to get his ass on stage and do the show that night, then Kevin would be the one to provide James with the therapeutic post-show massage and ice pack treatment that the doctor had required be performed in order to keep James' back from seizing up. There is no question or doubt that the intent of the good doctor's order was for a licensed professional massage therapist to perform this post-show duty but at this moment, circumstance dictated another choice. Kevin further stated to James, in that same life-changing moment, that he would be fine with doing this because the Olympics were being broadcast live from Seoul, Korea, with coverage starting at 11:00 p.m. They could watch the Olympics together while Kevin provided the required therapy to James' back.

James made it through the show, and Kevin and James returned to James' apartment, where Kevin began to very innocently give James the promised massage on the living room floor.

Not to go into too much detail, somewhere along the way of their last week in St. Louis, between the Olympic viewing hours of midnight and 2:00 a.m., with endless hours of very deep, no-subject-left-untouched conversation, having been given a doctor's "permission"—in fact, orders—for physical contact, that "next thing" between them happened. Their non-dating period of the last two months together had reached an inevitable and fully unplanned culmination—their new beginning.

But wait! But how? Kevin was married!

Kevin and James now found themselves in a relationship that neither of them could define, nor did they want to. It was hardest for Kevin, as the very idea of being in a relationship with another man for the first time in his life wasn't something he could wrap his mind around. Kevin's long-held conservative Christian beliefs told him this was a one-way ticket to Hell, but the need to follow his heart seemed to outweigh the fear. And for his part, James certainly wasn't looking to fall in love with a married man. Ironically, he had just completed a year of intense personal therapy, the focus of which had been dealing with his relationship issues and why, with the many wonderful men and women he had known, he still hadn't found the "one." At any rate, ideally matched or not, Kevin and James were blinded by their growing passion for one another and the real world outside of St. Louis simply didn't exist. They agreed that for both their sakes, and to prevent anyone from being hurt, secrecy was paramount. For one entire week, they lived in blissful denial of all reality.

The run of the show ended, and everybody headed home. It wasn't as if they had to say goodbye, as they both lived in New

York. They'd be seeing each other at the airport when they landed, and they'd already planned a bowling evening three days out. This would include James, Kevin, Kevin's wife, and five or six Candide cast members, with dinner and drinks to follow. Nevertheless, their last private, tearful conversation before departing St. Louis had been its own form of goodbye. Kevin was returning to his marriage, and James was returning to his life as an unattached single man in the big city. They were no longer lovers, just mere friends again. They didn't even sit together on the flight back to New York.

The first surreal moment came when, after picking their bags up off the luggage carousel, Kevin turned to greet his wife with a hug and a kiss, and James jumped into a waiting car. Kevin went home with his wife, and James returned to his own apartment.

Having a killer three-bedroom prewar apartment on the Upper West Side of Manhattan has its advantages, the best of which (for this story at least) was that James was able to convert the smallest of the bedrooms into a home gym. Not one to let a perfectly good idea go to waste, James thought it harmless and safe enough to call and ask if his workout buddy wanted to keep up the gym schedule they had created while in St. Louis, with the slight modification being that the gym was now located in James' apartment. Conning themselves (because of course they both unconsciously wanted to be conned), Kevin and James actually thought of this as an obvious and innocent way to stay connected as "friends." Just two guys, working out, alone, sweating . . . just two guys who had just days before been lovers, but who were no longer going to be lovers ever again.

Yeah, right!

And so, they rekindled their secret affair. The excitement, the passion, the sex, the intimacy, the connection, all offset by a slew of guilty thoughts: cheater, adulterer, betrayer, home-wrecker, immorality, sin, hell, damnation, pain, and sadness. This relationship was doomed, over before it had begun. It had nowhere to go.

For the next month, Kevin and James met almost daily for their "workouts." Their simple ruse seemed to fool everyone, from Kevin's wife to all their many friends. They were never long trysts, short enough to be believable, and on many occasions were not workouts at all but had morphed into walks in Central Park, going to a movie, and of course, bowling. The pain of deceiving others was actually not the most difficult part. It was the fact that they were fooling themselves, living a lie and having to put on more and more of a facade to keep the lie going.

Just as they had reached a point where the tension of the lie was threatening to shatter everyone's lives, James was mercifully cast in a show that was taking him out of town. The affair would end by default—the easy way out, but a way out nevertheless. The decision to end what had begun was made for them.

James was to have three weeks of rehearsals in New York before heading to Cleveland to play the part of Paul in Carnival. They agreed to make the most of their final three weeks together, and further agreed that this separation would be a return to normal, to the status quo, to the way it was before St. Louis.

To say goodbye, they hatched a plan by which they could spend one romantic night together. James had a dear friend who owned a wonderful old home not far from the ocean in Southampton. The final hurrah was to be an overnight trip, ostensibly to assist James' friend with the removal of a tree and whatever else he needed to have done. On James' last day off, just before he left to do the show, they headed off to Long Island. Emotions were riding high on the drive out and only continued to get heavier once they arrived. It was the first week of November, a weekday, and Southampton was quiet, the beaches nearly deserted but for the occasional dog and his walker. James and Kevin sat by the shore and then walked the beach for what must have been two or more hours. They discussed a future that might have been, but wouldn't be. The pain of admitting to being gay and leaving his wife wasn't going to happen for Kevin. Those thoughts collided with every belief he held in his mind, so contemplating dramatic life changes of this magnitude was simply too painful and out of the question. And so, this walk on the beach would be the end. The sun had started to set as they sat watching the ocean, mostly in silence. Then James handed Kevin a small, white, heart-shaped stone he'd found in the sand and said, "Hang on to this. If this stone can make it all the way here to this beach without turning into sand, then it's as strong as my love for you." Kevin handed James his own white stone to carry. Both stones wound up in their pockets as they sat and hugged and cried, watching the waves as they crashed on the shore at Flying Point Beach. Kevin and James had known each other three months and had been lovers for less than half that period. As James left town, they agreed not to speak or communicate for thirty days. The forced separation and self-imposed communication blackout was to be the cure and release for heartache. It was a good idea, and a sensible plan. Kevin returned to being a faithful husband and James left the city. Their love affair— their gay love affair—was done, and would be put in the past.

Thirty days went by, in which Kevin and James actually managed to keep their promise to have no contact with each other. On the thirtieth day, James bravely broke the radio silence and called Kevin at work. (Between theater jobs, Kevin maintained a temporary desk job to make money.) To James' shock and disappointment, Kevin was cold and distant. Even though Kevin had had his share of sadness and tears over the past month, he responded to James' "I miss you. Do you miss me? What have you been doing? I love you" with, "I'm fine, but I can't. I'm married and I want to stay married. I can't think of what any of it means. I just can't." Hearing this, James said, "Well, if we can't be together then we can't be friends." And with a final, "Take care . . . Goodbye," the conversation was over.

A week of torture followed for Kevin. He had stuck to his resolve to end the relationship, but his pain, self-doubt, and questions about his personal identity would not leave him alone. There seemed to be nothing that could happen that could resolve the untenable dilemma in which he found himself.

About a week after Kevin and James' "final" conversation, Kevin's agent called with a wonderful job offer. They were re-mounting a production of Jesus Christ Superstar in Chicago, and they wanted Kevin to reprise the role of Pontius Pilate, which he had done in a previous tour. The show would play for three months right after Christmas, and would be directed and choreographed by none other than his friend Terry, who had directed the production of Candide where Kevin had met James. Kevin, of course, loved working with Terry, so this was good news. Kevin's agent then went on to say, "Casting said to tell you that Jesus will be played by the guy you did Candide with in St. Louis. The bad news is that the producer is being cheap and insists that you be hired as a local Chicago actor. This means that the producer will not be providing you with a place to live. But the good news is, the producer will be providing the guy playing Jesus with a two-bedroom apartment, and he has agreed to let you live with him if you are interested and want to save money!"

Silence. . . . With the words "Are you kidding?" screaming in his head, alternating between excitement and dread, Kevin heard his agent say, "Helloooo?" "Yes," Kevin said, with no emotion. "Yes, what?" his agent said. "Yes!" said Kevin, only this time with pure excitement. "Are you kidding? Of course I'll do it!" Someone should have cued the fireworks, but with his wife watching TV in the next room, Kevin would have to make do with quiet celebration.

The phone rang again a few minutes later. Kevin answered, thinking it must be his agent calling with more details. This time it was James. "Well, what do you think? Are you OK with this?" Perhaps because James was older by six years, or maybe because he was more determined that the two of them be together, James always made the first move in those early years. James truly believed that this turn of events was perfect, and that there would be no problems with their sharing an apartment. To this day James is the ultimate idealist, and that can be a great frustration for a realist like Kevin. James wasted no time selling Kevin on the idea that doing Superstar in Chicago was the universe providing the circumstance for them to be together so they could focus all their energies on being good friends and nothing more. It's hard to imagine someone actually saying a line like that, but James did. And it's harder still to imagine someone actually believing a line like that, but Kevin did. The false efforts they'd made to "not" be together were overtaken by the truthful desire to "only" be with one another.

In the month of anticipation leading up to Chicago, there were many discussions over the phone planning and plotting how fun it was going to be, each time with the insistence that they would not re-open the door to their physical intimacy. Celebrating the Christmas holiday with his wife was a great acting challenge for Kevin. Did she suspect anything? Maybe she did. The thought of getting a divorce was still a distant second in Kevin's list of concerns, compared to any thought or acknowledgement that he could be gay. Prayers had stopped offering any relief, and in those quiet moments the guilt only worsened. The thought of betraying his wife, friends, family and God, all at the same time, only brought to mind questions like, "How could this ever end in a good way?"

The approaching holidays only served to increase Kevin's level of sadness. His wife asked him repeatedly that Christmas if anything was wrong. If she sensed it, perhaps even suspected what it was, she never let on. No doubt her own denial of the possibility that her husband might be gay was a far easier choice to make.

Kevin arrived in Chicago several days ahead of James, who was finishing the run of his show in Cleveland. This allowed Kevin to set up the small apartment and settle himself into the smaller of the two bedrooms. The moment of truth came several days later as Kevin and James sat facing one another on the apartment's living room couch. James, exhausted and newly arrived, had thrown his luggage in the empty, larger front bedroom. The hope of their being together had been let go of during the Southampton trip. But now, here they were. The many conversations and planning of what they'd intended to have happen in Chicago no longer mattered. All of that seemed irrelevant to what was being felt and shared. When you find someone and you fall in love—well, you know you are in love. The emotional connection had grown quickly and it had now only been five months. But there was a great deal more on the table, with this being Kevin's first gay relationship. If plans are meant to change and new paths are meant to be discovered, then that is exactly what happened in that moment. The choice of living together had already been made, and the short-term nature of this situation allowed that to happen without concern for the long-term. The safety of that moment allowed Kevin to accept being gay. The admission had been coming, but the full realization could only happen when the circumstance was right. That wintry afternoon on a couch in Chicago was a life-changing moment. A completely truthful moment, shared with his new best friend.

Coming out but still being married, accepting being gay, living together for the first time and sharing a bathroom, co-starring in a show, living in secrecy—that's a pretty full plate to the start of any relationship. It's funny to think of taking it one step at a time when reviewing that list. Elevators don't move that fast, forget about taking the stairs. James moved into the small bedroom that Kevin had set up for himself and they used his larger bedroom as nothing more than a closet. They were fully together from the first day they arrived in Chicago. A month would pass quickly, opening night would come and go with the expected fanfare, and everything was perfect.

There's an expression in theater: "On the road doesn't count." But it does, when you are still married and haven't actually come out to the one person whose life you are about to destroy in an instant.

Kevin's wife had come to Chicago for a visit which just happened to perfectly coincide with Valentine's Day. All three of them were now sharing the apartment for a long weekend. The tension was palpable at every turn, with discomfort on full display and denial making its last stand. Wife and good friend in one corner, new best friend, lover, and future husband in the other. The screaming and fighting was deafening, or would have been if anything had been said or truthfully spoken. But everyone held their silence. And as good stories go, it was on Valentine's Day, 1989, that Kevin found a card and wrote to James that he hoped this would be the last Valentine's Day they would ever spend apart. James would find that card neatly hidden beneath the pillow in his large front bedroom.

Shortly after that weekend, Kevin flew home one Sunday night to New York for the day off. Confessions were made, hearts were broken, and tears, many tears, were shared. Total truth at last.

Kevin and James believe they were soul mates by destiny, best friends who found each other this time around. As of today, they've been together twenty-eight years. Their careers have both expanded and intertwined to include not only acting but ministry, producing, and writing. They are the proud parents of twins who are now seventeen years of age, and they continue to enjoy working out, bowling and playing tennis together . . . without the white shorts, of course.

And they both still carry their white stones.

Friends First

In 1982, after having been a singer and an actress for fifteen years in Los Angeles, Kathie Lee was offered a job in New York on Good Morning America. The plan was to groom her to take over for Joan Lunden, who had been co-hosting the show for many years. Ordinarily, Kathie Lee would never have considered this. She was an actress and a singer, not a journalist. But she was going through a divorce and thought, "Maybe a change of scene would do me good." She figured she could go to New York, do the show for about a year, and move on.

Kathie Lee's first question when she arrived at the show was, "Why me? I have no background or experience in television journalism." But the powers that be had seen something special in her. Her personality. Her interest in people. Something undefinable. So they set out to groom her, teaching her how to do an interview, how to present guests, how to tell a news story—all the skills necessary to be a news program co-host. Kathie Lee was an open and willing student, and she learned fast and well.

One morning, at about 5 a.m., Kathie Lee arrived at the studio to film an Alpo dog food commercial with a Basset Hound. (One of the less glamorous parts of her job.) She was walking toward her dressing room when she passed another dressing room in which she saw a man leaning over the sink, putting in his contact lenses. To be more specific, what Kathie Lee actually saw was a pair of the tightest buns she'd ever seen belonging to a man she didn't know leaning over the sink putting in his contact lenses. That was her first glimpse of Frank Gifford. His "tight end."

Not long before, Kathie Lee had had an operation on her eyes called radial keratotomy. The precursor to Lasix, the operation was done with a razor blade, and the anesthesia used was liquid cocaine. It was absolutely primitive compared to the eye surgery we have today, but the result was that Kathie Lee went from being nearly legally blind to having perfect 20/20 vision, something that was essential for reading the teleprompter for the job she was now in.

Seeing this man she didn't know putting in contact lenses, Kathie Lee yelled in, "Have I got an operation for you!" to which he replied, "Yeah, with a fool on either end." Frank's doctor had warned him that anyone who opted to have that operation was a fool, and any doctor who agreed to perform it was an idiot.

Frank, who, of course, had not only been one of the greatest football stars who ever lived, but had been co-hosting Monday Night Football for years, was a very experienced TV sportscaster. On that particular morning, he had been brought in to sub for David Hartman as the host of Good Morning America.

From that first day, Kathie Lee and Frank hit it off and became friends. With Frank being twenty-three years Kathie Lee's senior, there was absolutely no thought of romance. But Frank became Kathie Lee's knight in shining armor, protecting her and looking after her. Once, when he saw her sitting in for Joan Lunden on Good Morning America, Frank called Kathie Lee and said, "Joan Lunden is much taller than you. You look like a chicken looking up at David Hartman when you're sitting in her chair. They should raise the chair for you." And he then called the producers and told them to give Kathie Lee a higher chair. Which they did.

(Kathie Lee says that in truth, it was just Frank's nature to be that way, and he did that sort of thing for a lot of people. He did the same thing for Caitlyn Jenner—then Bruce—when he was making the transition from athlete to sportscaster.)

For the next four years, Kathie Lee and Frank were friends. Frank would call her out of the blue and say, "The cowboy is in town!" (meaning his co-host, the wild and crazy Don Meredith) and invite Kathie Lee to lunch with the two of them. Kathie Lee would sit there in awe thinking, "I'm really out of my league. These are two of the greatest legends in the history of sports, and I'm sitting here having lunch with them."

What really amazed Kathie Lee was how interested these guys were in knowing about her. When they asked Kathie Lee how her life was going, she told them that she was coming off a divorce and dating a sweet guy. Don Meredith turned to her and said, "Kathie Lee, I'm sorry. You need to find yourself a really good man, someone who's going to look at you and say, 'I'm gonna take a tour of you from the top of your head to the tip of your toes with a lot of intermittent stops in between.'" "Oh boy," Kathie Lee thought, "I'm not in Kansas anymore!"

Soon after that lunch, Kathie Lee started dating another man. They broke up nine times within one year, and each time they broke up, Kathie Lee and Frank would get together for lunch and talk about it. Similarly, whenever Frank went through a crisis—when his brother died, when a pilot died in a private plane and Frank had tried to resuscitate him—Frank would call Kathie Lee to talk about it.

One day, Frank was listening to Kathie Lee tell him about her ninth breakup with the guy she was dating, and he suddenly said, "I'm sick of this. You're going to hang out with me until you are over this guy!"

From that day on they began seeing each other more frequently, still always as friends. Kathie Lee got herself a little house in the Hamptons, and since Frank often went out there to stay with his lawyer, they sometimes traveled out there together and would see each other during the weekend. The weekend of the 1986 US Open, Frank drove Kathie Lee out to the Hamptons for a party. When they got there, Frank said, "I'm going to say hello to a few people and I'll be back." Since there was nothing romantic going on between them, Kathie Lee of course thought nothing of it. Fifteen minutes later, Frank came back and said, "OK, I've done my duty. Now I've come home." Kathie Lee thought, "What an odd thing to say." But she liked it. It made her feel good.

At that party they were introduced to something called "The Music Box." A precursor to Karaoke, it would play just the track of a famous song, and would record your vocal performance. The track that came on was "You Don't Bring

Me Flowers," the song made famous by Barbra Streisand and Neil Diamond. Kathie Lee and Frank decided to do the duet together. Kathie Lee began, and being a professional singer, began really singing it. Then Frank came in, and his appalling lack of any sense of rhythm was hilarious to Kathie Lee. They did it over and over, each time getting more hysterical with laughter. The last time they sang it, Kathie Lee fell off the couch, and as she looked up at Frank from the floor she knew she was in love with him. (In fact, Kathie Lee still has that tape, so she literally has a recording of the moment she fell in love with Frank Gifford.)

That was June of 1986. They were married in October of the same year, and they stayed married until Frank's passing, two months shy of their twenty-ninth anniversary.

Through all those years, with all the pressures that two celebrity careers and the resultant life lived under the microscope of public scrutiny can bring, Kathie Lee and Frank Gifford navigated the waters of whatever came their way, had two wonderful kids together, and most of all, were friends from beginning to end.

In thinking back on it, Kathie Lee likes to say, "You don't find love. Love finds you."

Author's Afterword

Three years had gone by since my breakup and I was still single, not even able to get a date let alone meet a partner. I was more depressed than ever.

Norm Lewis, a great Broadway singer, called me up and asked if I had a piano copy of my song "We Can Be Kind" in his key. We had just performed it at the Duke Children's Hospital Benefit, but I had been at the piano so I hadn't written it out. I asked him why he needed it and he said he had been asked to sing at Unity of New York, a New Thought Church where many Broadway celebrities performed.

I had heard about Unity but had never been there, so I said, "I'll come down and play it for you."

We went down there, and I got a standing ovation for just walking in. Apparently they had been singing my songs at Unity for years, so my reputation preceded me. The performance was a big success, so I stayed for the sermon. I found it to be brilliant, comforting, and just what I needed, so I began riding my bicycle down to Unity every week and quietly sitting on the side, not talking to very many people, just soothing my soul.

A few weeks later I got a phone call. The voice on the message machine said, "Hi, David. I'm the music minister at Unity and

I'm sticking my neck out here because we don't know you very well, but we were wondering if we might hire you to sing and play on our annual retreat. The subject is Healing Your Heart."

"Hm," I thought. "Something I could use." So I said yes.

I went to that retreat thinking that in my head I wanted to heal and move on, but feeling that my heart was broken. In the course of the retreat, I came to understand that it wasn't my heart that was broken. A heart cannot be broken because it always contains the infinite possibilities of the universe. It was my head that was broken.

I was sitting quietly in a chapel at the retreat, meditating, when suddenly I had the thought, "Wait a minute. Patti LuPone must have auditioned for Cats, but she didn't get it because Betty Buckley got it. Patti didn't draw the conclusion from that one audition that she couldn't do a Broadway show. She went on to do many Broadway shows. Why am I drawing the conclusion from this one guy dumping me that I can't have a boyfriend? I'm a great guy. I would make someone a wonderful boyfriend."

And as I was thinking this, the door to the chapel opened and Shawn walked in and said, "Hi." He sat down and we started talking, and after about ten minutes I looked over at him and thought to myself, "This guy's hitting on me. I haven't seen that in years."

Shawn and I have been partners ever since. At this writing we're going on fifteen years together, and it gets better and better every year.

In looking at it, I realized that I had been going through the world thinking, "Nobody would want to date me." With that thought in mind, I was unable to notice anyone who might be interested in me. When I exchanged my thought, suddenly I was able to see someone who was interested.

To prove the point, Shawn told me that when he'd been introduced to me six years earlier at a memorial service (I do not remember meeting him there), he had looked in my eyes and said to himself, "This is the man for me. Someday we will be together." So he had been in love with me for the past six years, even when I had been with my previous boyfriend! It took a change in thought on my part to see what had been there all the time.

Author's Afterword

ORDER YOUR COMPANION CD AT
MIDDER2000@AOL.COM

At first glance, it might seem unusual for someone who's spent his whole career writing songs to suddenly put out a book of stories about how people met. In looking over the songs I've written, however, I realized that over the years, songs about longing for love, knowing that love is there, finding love, and treasuring the love we've found, have been constant themes for me. I have included a collection of these on a companion CD that I recorded specially to accompany this book. To increase your "total immersion" experience, I hope you will order the CD, listen to these songs, enjoy them, and be encouraged and inspired by them.

1. YOU'RE ALREADY THERE
   Music & Lyrics by David Friedman
   ©MIDDER Music Publishing, Inc. (ASCAP)

2. OPEN YOUR EYES TO LOVE
   (From the movie Trick)
   Music & Lyrics by David Friedman
   ©MIDDER Music Publishing, Inc. (ASCAP)/Walt Disney
   Music Company (ASCAP)

3. THERE IS LIFE
   (Written for Disney's Bambi II) Music & Lyrics by David
   Friedman ©MIDDER Music Publishing, Inc. (ASCAP)/
   Walt Disney Music Company (ASCAP)

4. DREAM BIGGER
    (Written for David Tutera's Dream Bigger Tour) Music &
    Lyrics by David Friedman
    ©MIDDER Music Publishing, Inc. (ASCAP)

5. I CAN HOLD YOU
    Music & Lyrics by David Friedman
    ©MIDDER Music Publishing, Inc. (ASCAP)

6. HELP IS ON THE WAY
    Music & Lyrics by David Friedman
    ©MIDDER Music Publishing, Inc. (ASCAP)

7. IT'S NEVER TOO LATE FOR LOVE
    (Written for The Today Show) Music by David Friedman
    ©MIDDER Music Publishing, Inc. (ASCAP)
    Lyric by Kathie Lee Gifford ©Cassy/Cody Music, Inc.
    (ASCAP)

8. I FINALLY LET GO
    Music & Lyrics by David Friedman
    ©MIDDER Music Publishing, Inc. (ASCAP)

9. TRICK OF FATE
    (Theme song from the movie Trick)
    Music & Lyrics by David Friedman
    ©MIDDER Music Publishing, Inc. (ASCAP)

10. COMING HOME
    Music by Jeff Franzel

©Bird Wins Music, Inc. (ASCAP)
Lyric by Barbara Rothstein ©Applesongs (ASCAP) &
David Friedman
©MIDDER Music Publishing, Inc. (ASCAP)

11. JUST IN TIME FOR CHRISTMAS
Music by David Friedman
©MIDDER Music Publishing, Inc. (ASCAP) Lyric by
David Zippel ©In Your Ear Music (ASCAP)

12. WHAT I WAS DREAMIN' OF
Music & Lyrics by David Friedman
©MIDDER Music Publishing, Inc. (ASCAP)

13. LISTEN TO MY HEART
Music & Lyrics by David Friedman
©MIDDER Music Publishing, Inc. (ASCAP)

14. IN YOUR EYES
Music by Jeff Franzel ©Bird Wins Music, Inc. (ASCAP)
Lyric by David Friedman
©MIDDER Music Publishing, Inc. (ASCAP)

15. YOUR LOVE
Music & Lyrics by David Friedman
©MIDDER Music Publishing, Inc. (ASCAP)

16. WE LIVE ON BORROWED TIME
Music & Lyrics by David Friedman
©MIDDER Music Publishing, Inc. (ASCAP)

17. I'LL BE HERE WITH YOU
    Music & Lyrics by David Friedman
    ©MIDDER Music Publishing, Inc. (ASCAP)

To order CDs or sheet music to any of these songs, write to MIDDER2000@aol.com.

To download the CD or recordings of any of these songs, go to itunes.com or amazon.com

If you have a great "How They Met" story of your own that you would like to share, please send it to MIDDER2000@ aol.com. Perhaps yours will appear if there is a next book!

About the Author

David Friedman, one of this country's most beloved songwriters, is best known for writing songs that touch our hearts and speak to our souls.

He has written songs for everyone from Disney to Diana Ross, produced all of the late/great Nancy LaMott's CD's and wrote many of her best known songs, conducted and vocal arranged six musicals on Broadway and numerous Disney Animated Films (including Beauty & The Beast, Aladdin, Pocahontas, and The Hunchback of Notre Dame), has performed his Off-Broadway revue Listen To My Heart: The Songs of David Friedman to audiences in New York City, all over America and abroad, contributed songs to The Lizzie McGuire Movie, Aladdin and the King of Thieves, Bambi II, and Trick, scored three television series, and is currently in his ninth year of co-writing (with Kathie Lee Gifford) and performing a song-a-month for The Today Show's "Everyone Has a Story" segment.

David's latest musical, Desperate Measures, cowritten with Peter Kellogg, has become a long running Off-Broadway hit in New York, and plans are in the work to bring it to cities around the world. A widely read metaphysics author, David's groundbreaking books, The Thought Exchange®: Overcoming Our Resistance to Living a SENSATIONAL Life, a sequel to that book, The Healing Power of "Negative" Thoughts and "Uncomfortable" Sensations, and an accompanying workbook, It's ALL Inside, have been read all over the world. His most recent book, We Can Be Kind: Healing Our World One Kindness at a Time, based on his hit song We Can Be Kind, along with an accompanying DVD of Nancy LaMott singing the song, became one of the most successful books in its category upon its release.

In addition to an extensive writing and performing career, David is a sought-after lecturer and teacher all over the United States on the subject of The Thought Exchange®, a metaphysical method he created for "going beyond positive thinking" to true healing and understanding. For more information on David's work, or on how to contact him, go to MIDDERMusic.com.

Made in United States
Orlando, FL
25 July 2023

35461513R00134